Martina Napolitano

Sasha Sokolov:
The Life and Work of the Russian "Proet"

Literatur und Kultur im mittleren und östlichen Europa

herausgegeben von Reinhard Ibler

ISSN 2195-1497

15 *Dmitry Shlapentokh*
    The Mongol Conquests in the Novels of Vasily Yan
    An Intellectual Biography
    ISBN 978-3-8382-1017-9

16 *Katharina Bauer*
    Liebe – Glaube – Russland:
    Russlandkonzeptionen im Schaffen Aleksej N. Tolstojs
    ISBN 978-3-8382-1182-4

17 *Magdalena Baran-Szołtys, Monika Glosowitz,*
    Aleksandra Konarzewska (eds.)
    Imagined Geographies
    Central European Spatial Narratives between 1984 and 2014
    ISBN 978-3-8382-1225-8

18 *Adam Jarosz*
    Der Spiegel und die Spiegelungen
    Über Geschlecht und Seele im Werk von Stanisław Przybyszewski
    ISBN 978-3-8382-1246-3

19 *Šárka Sladovníková*
    The Holocaust in Czechoslovak
    and Czech Feature Films
    ISBN 978-3-8382-1196-1

20 *Julia Spanberger*
    Grenzen und Grenzerfahrungen in den Texten Viktor Pelevins
    Eine Analyse seiner frühen Prosa
    ISBN 978-3-8382-1460-3

21 *Magda Dolinska-Rydzek*
    The Antichrist in Post-Soviet Russia:
    Transformations of an Ideomyth
    ISBN 978-3-8382-1545-7

Martina Napolitano

SASHA SOKOLOV: THE LIFE AND WORK OF THE RUSSIAN "PROET"

Bibliografische Information der Deutschen Nationalbibliothek
Die Deutsche Nationalbibliothek verzeichnet diese Publikation in der Deutschen Nationalbibliografie; detaillierte bibliografische Daten sind im Internet über http://dnb.d-nb.de abrufbar.

Bibliographic information published by the Deutsche Nationalbibliothek
Die Deutsche Nationalbibliothek lists this publication in the Deutsche Nationalbibliografie; detailed bibliographic data are available in the Internet at http://dnb.d-nb.de.

Cover picture: Sasha Sokolov, photo by Samuele Pellecchia. Printed with kind permission.

ISBN-13: 978-3-8382-1619-5
© *ibidem*-Verlag, Stuttgart 2022
Alle Rechte vorbehalten

Das Werk einschließlich aller seiner Teile ist urheberrechtlich geschützt. Jede Verwertung außerhalb der engen Grenzen des Urheberrechtsgesetzes ist ohne Zustimmung des Verlages unzulässig und strafbar. Dies gilt insbesondere für Vervielfältigungen, Übersetzungen, Mikroverfilmungen und elektronische Speicherformen sowie die Einspeicherung und Verarbeitung in elektronischen Systemen.

All rights reserved. No part of this publication may be reproduced, stored in or introduced into a retrieval system, or transmitted, in any form, or by any means (electronic, mechanical, photocopying, recording or otherwise) without the prior written permission of the publisher. Any person who does any unauthorized act in relation to this publication may be liable to criminal prosecution and civil claims for damages.

Printed in the EU

Table of Contents

Introduction 7
Acknowledgements 13

Chapter 1. *Masquerade*, or "Maintain your reputation!" 17
    The son of the *nomenklatura* 18
    An asocial profile in the Moscow underground scene 21
    Fleeing the city 22
    Getting ready to leave 27
    A stopover in Vienna 29
    A North-American nomad 32
    Sasha Sokolov, the lecturer 36
    Soviet Union, *toccata and fugue* 40
    "An eternal student of the globetrotting department" 42

Chapter 2. *On Early Trains*, or Beyond Sasha Sokolov's Twilight Cosmos 51
    Emotional proximity 52
    Classification difficulty 56
    Close reading attempts 60
    Sasha Sokolov's baroqueness 82

Chapter 3. Pictures from an Exhibition 87
    A language to compose texts 88
    A sound architecture 95
    Triptych's music 100
    Voices on stage 114
    Triptych's "theatre of pure reason" 121

Chapter 4. Theory and Play of *Proeziia* 133
    A long *proetic* tradition 134
    A choice of awareness 138
    A baroque macro-genre 140

In Lieu of a Conclusion 145
References 151

Introduction

This book explores the poetics of one of the most significant Russian authors of the 20th century. Sasha Sokolov's oeuvre represents a milestone in the development of Russian literature. His legacy can be traced in much of the poetry and prose appearing in post-Soviet Russia. Taking the studies and analyses proposed so far as points of departure, these four chapters examine the keystones and the theoretical framework that arise from a close reading of Sokolov's works. This project endeavors to systematize the findings into what can be considered as a structured authorial theory of literary creation.

While "arguably the most important living Russian writer" (Boguslawski 2012: vii), Sasha Sokolov cannot be considered a prolific author. His first novel *A School for Fools* was published in 1976 by Carl Proffer's Ardis, as the writer fled the Soviet regime and landed in the United States. The book was an international success and was immediately translated into multiple languages. However, in 1980, his second novel *Between Dog and Wolf* met with less success. Due to the linguistic difficulties encountered in the reading process it has long challenged any translation attempt (the English version of this 'Russian *Finnegans Wake*' came out in 2017). Finally, in 1985, Sokolov's third and last novel *Palisandriia* (known in English as *Astrophobia*) was released.

In the writer's view, *Palisandriia* "would [have ended] the novel as a genre" (Johnson 1987a: 217): the assertion became a self-fulfilling prophecy, as Sokolov eschewed longform writing in order to concentrate instead on the development of a theoretical framework and on the practice of what he defines as *proeziia*. While this term and concept is frequently and haphazardly employed by critics, it has not been the subject of systematic analysis.

As one who was always drawn to isolation and wilderness, after *Palisandriia*'s publication Sasha Sokolov gradually disappeared from the literary public scene. His withdrawal from public life has led commentators to compare his figure to that of J.D. Salinger. However, after a set of lyric essays, Sokolov suddenly reappeared in the 2000s, authoring short compositions published by the Israeli Russian-language magazine "Zerkalo". These texts include three pieces later compiled in 2011 by the Moscow publishing house OGI: this *Triptych* is Sasha

Sokolov's fourth and last published book (excluding the collections of his complete works; 1999, 2020).

While Sasha Sokolov has authored a limited number of publications throughout his literary career, his oeuvre has inspired an impressive mass of critical articles and dissertations. Many analyses have been completed, especially in the United States in the 1980s and more recently, in Russia and Europe, mainly Italy. However, apart from published dissertations, no monograph has appeared, thus suggesting a heterogeneous yet fragmentary corpus of critical accounts.

In spite of the fact that articles have investigated many different aspects of Sokolov's novels, authors have failed to provide comprehensive overviews of the writer's poetics due to the limited size and scope of these publications. Moreover, while most investigations consider Sokolov's first masterpiece, limited attention has been dedicated to his recent *Triptych*. The situation is rather contradictory given the recognized role played by Sasha Sokolov in 20th-century and contemporary Russian literature.

Therefore, the purpose of this book is to propose the first systematic and longitudinal study of Sasha Sokolov's poetics. Zooming out from the specific stylistic and formal traits of his writing, this book, which is founded on my doctoral thesis (defended in March 2020 at the University of Udine, Italy), seeks to grasp the overall structure and message of Sasha Sokolov's hermetic literary works. Benefiting from a close personal exchange of ideas with the writer, the study presents a groundbreaking exploration of the fundamental tenets that underpin Sokolov's meaningful role as a literary creator of Beauty.

The book deals first and foremost with what has been regarded by critics as the central axis in the writer's literary cosmos: language. In support of this goal, the book takes the entire corpus of Sasha Sokolov's literary works into consideration, but concentrates primarily on *Triptych,* which is treated as his most mature and developed text.

This book aims to shed light on two significant and interrelated issues: first, the genesis and outcomes of Sokolov's linguistic mastery, and, second, the theoretical framework developed by the writer in relation to his definition of *proeziia*. Throughout the history of literature and in Russian culture in particular, theory and practice have been deeply intertwined. Reflection on the notion of genre often complements and accompanies the 'manufacturing' of an artistic object; in other words, literary theory and practice often develop in tandem in the work of Russian 'writers-theorists' (or 'writers-philosophers', as is the case, for example, of Lev Tolstoy).

While the application of tools derived from other texts or even disciplines can be fascinating, it also risks being misleading and diverting attention away from the keys intrinsic to the text. From the perspective of the literary criticism produced within the framework of Russian Formalism and later developed by the Moscow-Tartu School of Semiotics, this analysis stems from a close reading of Sokolov's texts, highlighting those elements that determine the form and content of the author's work.

The frequent exchange of ideas with the writer over the course of a multi-year period of correspondence supports the ideas and authorial assumptions drawn from textual analysis. A comparable 'emotional proximity' has characterized the work and biographical profile of the most prominent scholars of Sasha Sokolov's oeuvre: Donald Barton Johnson, Olga Matich, Alexander Zholkovsky, and Alexander Boguslawski have all entertained a personal relationship and correspondence with Sokolov, which is arguably essential to access the literary cosmos of such an eclectic author.

The book is divided into four main chapters followed by a conclusion. The first two chapters frame the writer's profile and work by situating it in the overall literary context, presenting its key traits, and narrating its reception. The following two chapters represent the core of the analysis, which is rooted in a detailed investigation of Sokolov's language and based primarily on the textual material of his *Triptych*. While the third chapter delves into the idiosyncratic linguistic practice proposed by Sokolov (its background and results), the fourth chapter explains the theoretical reflection that supports this practice and outlines a definition of the author's notion of *proeziia*.

Chapter 1 opens the investigation with an updated literary biography of Sasha Sokolov, which complements the previous biographies drafted by D.B. Johnson in 1987 and by Ludmilla Litus in 2006. The portrayal of Sokolov's histrionic yet introverted personality helps the reader to perceive the content and main stylistic features of Sokolov's literary works, *Triptych* included. The title of the chapter, *Masquerade, or "Maintain your reputation!"*, alludes to Mikhail Lermontov's renowned verse play (1835) in which the author depicted human life as a theatrical performance carried out by masks rather than real individuals. Such a view reflects Sokolov's profile, as he consciously put on a literary mask, even upon assuming his "pseudo-name" Sasha (Dark 1992: 225). In addition, the title quotes the writer's short essay *About the Other Encounter* (2006), in which he underlined the need for the artist to "maintain one's reputation" (2012: 77), thus continuing to play the role that has been taken on.

The volume continues by drawing upon the critical research pioneered by D.B. Johnson, Alexander Boguslawski, Olga Matich, and Alexander Zholkovsky (mainly in the 1980s). The second chapter summarizes the main interpretations advanced by scholars of Sokolov's oeuvre, among which Johnson's depiction of a structured "Twilight Cosmos" represents an especially lucid proposal. The title of Chapter 2, *On Early Trains, or Beyond Sasha Sokolov's Twilight Cosmos*, refers to this study. The other allusion is to a poem by Boris Pasternak which, besides being indirectly mentioned by Sokolov in the essay *The Shared Notebook* (1989), highlights both the pervasiveness of intertextuality in the writer's literary activity (and consequently in the critics' writings) and the central role of the train image as one of Sokolov's favorite literary motifs. This innovative chapter does not merely enumerate the various findings presented so far, but applies a critical approach to these interpretations while further elaborating new ideas. Among them, the notion of Baroque, as suggested by some critics, serves as a basis for structuring a clearer idea of 'Sokolovian baroqueness'.

Chapter 3 demonstrates that Sokolov's oeuvre must be understood within the wider framework of inter-artistic creation: the writer, a "failed composer" as he himself admits (Kochetkova 2017), in his literary work has tried to draw natural and spontaneous connections between artistic realms that are traditionally separated—word, sound, painting, performance. The title *Pictures from an Exhibition* derives from a section of Sasha Sokolov's second novel, *Between Dog and Wolf*, but it is in itself an intertextual reference to Modest Mussorgsky's homonym piano suite (1874), which underscores the conceptual link between different art forms. Although critics have frequently observed the idiosyncratic use of the Russian language employed in Sokolov's texts and the consequent difficulties encountered in the reading (and translating) process, a systematic investigation of such a linguistic game is lacking. Therefore, the third chapter assesses the role of language in Sasha Sokolov's oeuvre and its specific functions according to the writer's poetics. On the one hand, it identifies the authorial theoretical framework within which language is mastered in the texts, while on the other it explores the outcomes of Sasha Sokolov's word weaving. While the first part of the investigation suggests the existence of a direct link between the poetic word and music in Sokolov's cosmos, the second part highlights the importance of performance art in concretizing verbal music. The material analyzed in this section includes all of Sokolov's texts with special emphasis on *Triptych,* taken here as the writer's ultimate 'manifesto' of literary creation.

Finally, the book offers the first complete analysis of Sokolov's concept of *proeziia*. *Proeziia* is not merely a genre or style of Sokolov's creation, but a nuanced theoretical reflection on the role and value of literature, art, creation, and ultimately Beauty. That is to say, it is a reflection upon that notion of *iziashchnoe* (finesse) that turned into a keyword in *Triptych*. In 1989, Sokolov affirmed: "The time has come for a new period of synthesis. As I explained, genre interests me less than the kinds of works I write. I create *proetry* (*proeziia*)" (Podshivalov 2006: 352). Chapter 4 further clarifies the definition of Sokolov's neologism, highlighting its practical role as a stylistic reference point, its 'spiritual' value for self-identification and self-positioning in the wider literary and artistic context, and its theoretical meaning as a macro-genre. The title of this final section, *Theory and Play of Proeziia*, recalls the famous essay devoted to the *Duende* by Federico García Lorca, a poet Sokolov deeply admires.

The book's Conclusion discusses the findings of the last two chapters and their implication for what can be defined as a structured authorial theory of literary creation. Arguing that Sokolov's oeuvre must be reconsidered in light of inter-artistic creation, the general argument is that the interplay of form and content suggests a more comprehensive view on the meaning and value of Beauty. According to the writer, in its singular reflecting, interpreting and decoding of the world, art naturally tends toward the universal criterion of harmony.

Acknowledgements

A famous, deeply inspiring quote from the historian Carlo Ginzburg is "the risk of conducting a research lies in finding *only* what we seek." What Ginzburg means by this is that the most productive discoveries often happen by accident, when we come across unexpected stimuli, what he calls 'clues', suggestions that give our research a different twist, or raise a question we had not explored before. I was redirected to the path of Sasha Sokolov thanks to 'clues'. I came across this writer by chance when I was writing a master's thesis on Venedikt Yerofeyev; of course, I had heard of him before, but it was only then, in the most famous bookstore in Moscow, that I 'stumbled' across his second novel, *Between Dog and Wolf*, which immediately fascinated me. So much so that, a few years later I wrote and defended a dissertation on his most recent book, *Triptych*. However, these 'clues' would not have led to such a solid foundation for the present book if I had not benefited from the invaluable help, advice, support and (constant!) revision of my supervisor at the University of Udine, Professor Raffaella Faggionato, to whom I offer my utmost gratitude.

I am infinitely grateful to Sasha Sokolov for his patience, understanding and openness and indebted to him for his help in writing this book. Our personal exchanges, as well as the opportunity to consult the letters preserved in the Sokolov Collection of the University of Santa Barbara in California allowed me to get closer to this writer on a personal level. I extend a special thanks to the Sokolov Collection staff. Together, these exchanges allowed me to glimpse the author's lively personality, his irony and lightness, as well as his idiosyncratic use of language—and of the pencil: please take a look at Sasha's drawing of the exquisite landscapes in Bezborodovo on the Volga, which he sent me on December 24, 2018 (on page 15).

For various reasons, I would like to express my gratitude to Artiom Skvortsov, Maksim Amelin, Tatiana Kasatkina, Mario Caramitti, Anna Giust, Elisa Baglioni, Noemi Albanese, José Vergara. The inspiring exchange of thoughts and ideas with them, which took place in many different venues over the past years, from conferences to informal outings and dinners (including a very special New Year's Eve in Moscow: thank you Maksim!), has found its reflection in this book.

Special thanks to Professor Reinhard Ibler for appreciating my proposal and including the book in his Ibidem Verlag's series "Literature and Culture in Middle and Eastern Europe", and thanks to the editors for the excellent handling of the publication process.

Heartfelt thanks to Grace Sewell for the thorough proofreading of the manuscript and for her pertinent remarks and suggestions.

I dedicate this work to those who are here, and to those who are no longer, but always will be.

перевоз
деревня Новомелково
127-й км
село Едимново
деревня Горки
Волга →
Тверь
Ленинградское шоссе
деревня Низовка (затоплена)
мой кордон
на нерестилище ≈8 минут
Волга → г.Конаково
лодки
комплекс отдыха Завидово (см.Инет)
р.Шоша
Завидово
Безбородово
мост

Chapter 1.
Masquerade, or "Maintain your reputation!"

> "Marina! I know it—I am living for the last time."
> Marina Tsvetaeva, *The Tale of Sonechka*

In a recent documentary, the "last Russian writer" (*Sasha Sokolov. Poslednii russkii pisatel'*, 2017) first introduces himself simply as Alex, a "friend of the Sokolov family." Only after a few minutes does Sasha Sokolov reveal his true identity. The film, which was broadcast by Channel One Russia (*Pervyi kanal*) shortly after its release, not only reconstructs Sokolov's life stages, relationships, and personality traits, but also offers a glimpse—albeit incomplete, and perhaps largely pre-arranged by the writer himself—of his life today. Sokolov lives now in Canada with his fifth wife Marlene Royle, a professional rowing coach and former U.S. National Team rower, where he was born in 1943, amid the snowy and silent mountains he regularly traverses on his cross-country skis.

Thanks to numerous interviews, audio and video recordings, letters, and biographies (Johnson 1987a; Litus 2006), we know quite a bit about Sasha Sokolov's life and temperament. What emerges from this material, however, is the profile of a hybrid character, a constructed mask who continues to elude any fixed location, who refuses stability and classification, and who has cultivated a sketchy, anecdotal image of himself, a playful attitude he has cultivated even toward his own name.

Aleksandr Vsevolodovich Sokolov is the name on his Soviet passport, which he used to write his first publications in the late 1960s and early 1970s when he was enrolled at Moscow State University, and in the period immediately after. However, the writer has gone by the name Sasha Sokolov at least since 1976, when Ardis published *Shkola dlia durakov* (A School for Fools), arguably his most successful masterpiece.[1]

This chapter will briefly trace the life of Sasha Sokolov, updating the literary biography written by Donald Barton Johnson in 1987 and expanded by Ludmilla

---

[1] In this book, original Russian titles are given only the first time they are mentioned. Otherwise, the English translation will be used. This rule does not apply to Sasha Sokolov's third novel *Palisandriia*, which was translated in English with the adapted, and thus possibly misleading, title *Astrophobia*.

Litus in 2006. The following pages will sketch an idea of Sokolov's histrionic yet reserved personality in addition to examining the content and main stylistic features of his literary work.

The son of the *nomenklatura*

Like his future "Kremlin orphan"-hero Palisandr Dal'berg, Sokolov was born a child of the Soviet *nomenklatura* and grew up in restrictive conditions that did not suit him. As such, a deep need for freedom tormented him since childhood.[2] The urge to establish an independent life led him to gradually sever his familial and social ties.

As a child, Sokolov was forced to move with his family from his native Ottawa to Moscow in December 1947 as a result of the *Gouzenko affair* in 1945 (one of the key episodes that launched the Cold War) (Knight 2006); his father was an important Soviet spy.

The writer acknowledges the significant impact that the two cities, Ottawa and Moscow, had on him, especially on a linguistic level. Until the age of three, he does not seem to have uttered a word, confused by the bilingual or even trilingual context (Canadian bilingualism in addition to the Russian spoken at home) in which he found himself (Vrubel'-Golubkina 2011). Moreover, after the family moved, he did not feel welcomed by Moscow, a city that rejected him architecturally and socially. However, Sokolov also recounts happy moments related to his childhood, such as holidays in Crimea and in Ukraine, where his mother took him to all the 'Gogol places'. Indeed, Gogol is a writer for whom Sasha later developed the same admiration as his mother (Slepynin 2007).[3]

In the Sokol district of Moscow, where the Sokolov family was assigned, by a bizarre coincidence, an apartment in the early 1950s, the nearby cemetery and morgue became morbid attractions to the young Sasha. His strange passion for death and for the dead led him to work as an attendant in the morgue in 1961,

---

[2] The writer maintained: "From society I basically demanded one thing: to leave me alone" (Caramitti 2004a: 12). All translations are mine unless otherwise stated.
[3] In addition to the passion for Nikolai Gogol, from his mother and aunt the young Sokolov inherited some knowledge of the songs and fairy tales from Siberia that the two women—natives of this region—sang and narrated to him during childhood (Vrubel'-Golubkina 2011).

shortly before he enrolled at the Military Institute of Foreign Languages at his father's request (1962-1965).

Death, usually considered taboo in everyday life and relegated to specific places and moments, for Sokolov simply represents "one of the forms of our eternity" (Vrubel'-Golubkina 2011). Death is fundamental to our understanding of reality, and therefore it constitutes one of the central cores of the writer's poetics. Sokolov rejects the linear view of existence that characterizes modern civilization. Instead, he favors the cyclical models typical of archaic civilizations and oriental teachings, which define death as an organic phenomenon that follows a circular movement towards rebirth (Boguslawski 1987: 231). The boundaries between life and death blur in Sokolov's texts, as his characters interact with the living (Pavel Norvegov in *A School for Fools*) or write letters (Ilya Zynzyrela in *Mezhdu sobakoi i volkom*, Between Dog and Wolf) even in death. The circularity of time not only explains Palisandr Dal'berg's *déjà vu* experiences but also generates the "memories of the future" in *Palisandriia*.[4]

Along with death, madness (real? fictional? feigned?) is a recurring element in the writer's life and oeuvre. At primary school, the young Aleksandr, who began at an early age to write parodies and epigrams about teachers that were popular with his classmates, showed a temperament that was difficult to reconcile with strict Soviet discipline. From the beginning there was talk of his possible transfer to special education classes (that "school for fools" that his fictional "student so-and-so" attended), which never occurred. However, in the autumn of 1962, Sokolov indeed spent three months in a psychiatric hospital (Kashchenko Institute),[5] having convincingly simulated mental illness in order to avoid military

---

[4] Moreover, several times in Sasha Sokolov's literary biography, death has played a key role. For example, the death of the Communist Party Secretary Yuri Andropov, a central character in the epic-parody *Palisandriia*, forced the writer to revise the book just before publication. The constant toasts to his health proved futile (Matveev 2015), and his successor Konstantin Chernenko also passed away before the book was published. In his essay, *Portret russkogo khudozhnika v Amerike—V ozhidanii Nobelia* (A Portrait of an Artist in America—Waiting for the Nobel, 1986) the writer declared: poetry in Russia— and only in Russia, he repeatedly emphasized (Matich 1984: 222)—is a matter of life and death. Sometimes, this statement becomes literally true.

[5] It should be noted that until Gorbachev's perestroika, psychiatric hospitals were under the auspices of the Ministry of Internal Affairs instead of the Ministry of Health. As a result,

service: on that occasion, he claimed—persuasively, we shall assume—to be a drum, a harp, or an unexploded bomb.

According to Sokolov, madness, just like death, should be brought back into everyday life, thus unmasking the pretentiousness of our social order that attempts to hide it in predefined spaces and categories. The writer pokes fun at this attitude by simulating infirmity to his own advantage, questioning the authority that allegedly distinguishes what is insane from what appears rational. Sokolov viscerally doubts the material consistency of reality: "I have always felt the unreality of our reality; in general, I have always doubted it," he affirms in the aforementioned documentary. This statement echoes the words of many of his fictional characters, especially those that the "student so-and-so" devotes to the arbitrariness and artificiality of calendars and of our measurement of time:

> Our calendars are too arbitrary and the numbers written in them mean nothing and are backed by nothing, like counterfeit money. Why, for example, it is customary to think the first of January is followed by the second and not immediately by the twenty-eighth? Yes, and can days actually follow each other? This sequence of days is some poetic gibberish. There is no sequence at all; the days come whenever each feels like it, and occasionally several come simultaneously. And every often so a day does not come for a long time; in such a case one lives in emptiness, understands nothing, and is very sick (2015: 24-25).

All of Sokolov's characters are afflicted by real or perceived mental illness, by excesses of their *ego*, by emotional and/or physical dysfunction. Paradigmatic in this sense is also the "old navigator" (*Staryi shturman*), the protagonist of the short story that in 1971 secured Sokòlov his first prize in a literary contest. This competition was organized by "Nasha zhizn'", a newspaper devoted to the world of the visually impaired and blind. With this short text, the young Aleksandr Sokolov won 100 rubles for "the best short story about blind people."[6]

---

they were also frequently used as places of detention and 'correction' for intellectuals and dissidents.

[6] Sasha Sokolov stated in this regard: "Unfortunately, the editor at "Nasha zhizn'" considerably mutilated the text, and in over half a century I have tried not to think about it; however, the prize money was very welcome. As far as I remember, I went with some friends to the Sandunovskie baths and spent there the entire sum" (Personal communication, email, December 30, 2018).

An asocial profile in the Moscow underground scene

After completing the Military Institute and being released from the psychiatric hospital, Sokolov briefly joined the underground group known as SMOG (some of these friendships, especially that with Vladimir Aleinikov, would last over time). Sokolov coincidentally met the group's future members long before the SMOG group was 'officially' born: the evening he left the mental asylum, he was captivated by the young aspiring poets as they read verses aloud under the statue of the great poet in Mayakovsky Square. From then on, the future writer became a frequent attendee of these unofficial Saturday night readings. The group did not officially form until 1965, under the playful and polysemous acronym SMOG.[7] These young poets and artists, including Vladimir Aleinikov, Yuri Kublanovskii, Arkadii Pakhomov, Vladimir Batshev, and the painter Nikolai Nedbailo, revolved primarily around the profile of the poet Leonid Gubanov. They aspired to take up the legacy of the Avant-Garde and Futurism, in particular that of Mayakovsky, in whose shadow they gathered.

However, the group was forced to disband soon after its inception in September 1965, when public readings were banned by the authorities and the *smogisty* were 'punished': Gubanov was sent to a psychiatric facility, Aleinikov was expelled from Moscow State University, Batshev and Nedbailo were sent to Siberia. The group left behind a few samizdat publications, including the SMOG Manifesto.

Sokolov's essay *Obshchaia tetrad', ili zhe Gruppovoi portret SMOGa* (The Shared Notebook, or a Group Portrait of SMOG) was written years later, in the winter of 1989, after a chance meeting with Aleinikov's wife in Belgrade. This interesting text subtly conceals the names and some of the works of the *smogisty*, especially those concerning Gubanov and Aleinikov. Being an authentic lyrical composition, Sokolov's essay portrays the emotional and spiritual experience of self-discovery as poets and artists through a series of interconnected images, each blurring into the contours of the other: in such a neglected and clandestine artistic

---

[7] It can be interpreted as Samoe Molodoe Obshchestvo Geniev (The Youngest Society of Genies), Smelost' Mysl' Obraz Glubina (Courage Thought Image Depth), Szhatyi Mir Otrazhennoi Giperboly (Compressed World of the Reflected Hyperbole), or as the past tense of the verb *smoc'* (I could, I dared).

world, they exploded "in the manner of the distant suns" (2012: 51). The collage structure of the text—a kind of cento—emphasizes the collective element of this awakening, the mutual discovery and inspiration, the common search for new forms and new models. At the same time, it highlights how each member of this "group portrait" represented an individual poetic nucleus within the "shared notebook" of this artistic experience (Napolitano 2020a).

Sokolov was not directly affected by the group's forced dissolution in September 1965, having already distanced himself from it. He no longer desired to participate in the evenings of the *smogisty*: "I did not understand how they could compose in such an atmosphere—there was music in the apartment, people talked, discussed.... Soon I got tired of it all and left" (Slepynin 2007). Sokolov distanced himself from the SMOG experience in order to work in solitude and escape from socially suffocating contexts (in this interview he defined himself as an "asocial" person). An irrepressible urge for freedom soon took him far away from Moscow, this 'infernal' nucleus (similar to Venichka Yerofeyev's Moscow) with an unstoppable centrifugal force.

Fleeing the city

In 1966 Sokolov enrolled in the Faculty of Journalism at MGU, which he defined as the "freest institution at the time, if we exclude mental asylums." In the same interview, the writer mentioned Yasen Nikolaevich Zasurskii, the only dean in USSR who was not a member of the Communist party—"we were allowed to discuss anything we wanted in class," samizdat included, he stated (Vrubel'-Golubkina 2011).

Sokolov began to collaborate with various newspapers in 1967: journalistic writing served as a testing ground for him, especially on the formal and stylistic level. During college, Sokolov took advantage of fieldwork opportunities, in particular in northern Siberia (Krasnoyarsk krai), where he collected stories of workers and pioneers that he later published in the faculty magazine "Studencheskii meridian" and in the almanac "Ballada o tret'em semestre" (1971). In this almanac thirteen short articles are authored by Aleksandr Sokolov; they all contain a fascinating mixture of Soviet clericalism and poetic elements.

In 1968 Sokolov eventually chose to register as a non-attending student (*zaochnoe obuchenie*) due to his frustration with city life. He moved to the village of Morki in the Mari Autonomous Soviet Socialist Republic with Taisiia Suvorova, a fellow student and his first wife until 1974.

He then concluded his studies in 1971, having already started to collaborate with the prestigious "Literaturnaia gazeta" mainly submitting book and art reviews. His last article published on the pages of this weekly magazine, titled *Poznat' prirodu tetivy* (Knowing the nature of the bowstring), was dedicated to Mari poets. In this text, Sokolov expressed his appreciation for the first translations that appeared in Russian, but also included general reflections concerning poetry and art—"Let us compare the poet's gift to a magic bow, invisible to an external eye, and let's compare the poet's verse to the string, which is stretched more or less sonorously depending on the quality of the wood of the limbs" (1971: 18).

Shortly thereafter, however, Sokolov could no longer bear living in the capital and sought refuge elsewhere:

> I had to find somewhere to live and think. I remembered a beautiful location north of Moscow, on the Volga. A school friend, more exactly his family, had a dacha there, next to a hunting estate and a small village. We had been going there for a long time during winter and summer. I rented a small *izba* for ten rubles a month. The owner arranged for me to work as a gamekeeper: I already knew something about hunting. The work was not particularly burdensome, I had some free time (Vrubel'-Golubkina 2011).

Sokolov spent the period between May 1972 and November 1973 at the hunting estate located near Bezborodovo in the Kalinin oblast (today Tver). These months constitute one of the most significant periods in the writer's life. In Bezborodovo, Sokolov not only wrote his first novel, but collected material that would become fundamental for his later work.

The inexorable search for seclusion would represent a constant in Sokolov's life: even after emigrating, he disliked attending conferences and conventions, as well as participating in formal meetings with other writers.[8] Such an escape from

---

[8] In a letter addressed to his publisher Carl Proffer, who suggested that he maintained good social ties after emigrating, Sokolov wrote: "As far as I am concerned, I have decided that I will no longer participate in events of this kind [he had just participated in the European Forum Alpbach]: I do not speak well, and in general there is very little sense in it all" (Mss

urban and social places further distanced the writer from his previous identity as the Soviet citizen Aleksandr Sokolov, as he definitely became Sasha Sokolov while writing *A School for Fools* in Bezborodovo.

Far away from the capital city, the writer achieved his childhood dream to become a *lesovik*—the faun, the spirit, or the man of the forest according to East Slavic folklore (Boguslawski 1987: 240), immersing himself in nature just like his fictional characters do: the "student so-and-so" metamorphoses into a Nymphaea alba; *Triptych*'s widow transfigures into a desperate and annoying fly; Palisandr's name implicitly recalls the immortal rosewood tree (*palisandr* in Russian). Transfiguration, metamorphosis, emigration—the latter broadly interpreted as the abandonment of one context and the passage to another, however intermediate and changeable—are images often associated, in the writer's essays, with the defamiliarizing discovery of the poetic element in oneself. In other words, the poet discovers his own poetic touch experiencing a nearly epiphanic moment—not by chance, the title of the essay dedicated to the centenary of Boris Pasternak's birth is *Znak ozaren'ia* (A Mark of Illumination, 1991). Thus, the poet literally metamorphoses: originally an "anxious pupa" (*trevozhnaia kukolka* in a Sokolov's homonym essay, 1986), he turns into a humble "slave of [...] language" (2012: 38).

This transformation process is also linked to a shift from the determinate to the indeterminate. Palisandr Dal'berg is, for example, an androgynous figure, a hermaphrodite, who in the course of the narrative switches, even in grammatical gender, from masculine to neuter. Moreover, given that distinctions between content and form no longer exist, Sokolov's narrative genre also reflects a kind of formal indeterminacy—Sokolov coined the term *proeziia* in this regard. After all, Russia for Sokolov is *inter canem et lupum* (between dog and wolf)[9], which is to say an essentially indeterminate space. As the writer himself explained:

117, Box 1: 5-6). When he later had the opportunity to meet Vladimir Nabokov in Switzerland (their mutual admiration is well known), he declined, claiming that he would have not known what to say to him.

[9] The Latin expression entered the Russian language through French, being immortalized in Pushkin's *Eugene Onegin*. Vladimir Nabokov allegedly suggested to Sokolov—through a letter to Ardis—that such expression was used in Pushkin's masterpiece (Erofeev 1989: 198).

> Russia is in many ways an indeterminate and unpredictable country. Especially the deep Russian province, peasant Russia. Everything there is somewhat imprecise and indefinite. And you never know how things will change in the aftermath. You cannot be sure of anything, of anyone, of any relationship. What is promised can be waited for three years, or maybe until the second coming. Time is usually not a limit. It is not fashionable to wear a watch. Today's friend can suddenly become your enemy. Or the other way around. The indeterminacy of reality is also reflected in our language. We, writers, do not cease to delight in the Russian language. We praise its flexibility and freedom. In Russian, the order of the sentence follows practically no rules, everything is left to arbitrariness. It is this general imprecision and lack of focus on Russian reality and language that is reflected in my novel [*Between Dog and Wolf*] (Caramitti 2004a: 12).

Indeed, in Russia natural boundaries are easily erased: snow covers roads and delimitations, ice freezes rivers and joins previously disjointed banks (a cardinal condition in *Between Dog and Wolf*), the vast steppe and the infinite taiga offer no obstacles to the eye, while the Volga river inexorably flows and submerges islands—such as the one near Bezborodovo, where Rilke's translator and poet Spiridon Drozhzhin[10] once lived. Whether as a blessing or a curse, as fate or refuge, the Russian space has played a specific role in Russian literature, and Sokolov's oeuvre is not devoid of reflection on this peculiar geography.

The establishment of Soviet rule and the consequent centralization of power in the old-new capital city Moscow marked a decisive shift in Russian geography. A new, molded mental map derived, which envisioned a concentric system rotating around Moscow. The countryside became an isolated place with no contact with either the center or the periphery. The province found itself affected by a 'storm of violence', emerging thereafter as a greatly impoverished land, a territory deprived of all its vital energy[11] (Schlögel 2016). Such was also the Bezborodovo area Sokolov lived in, a "world of casual violence, generally alcoholic" (Johnson 1987a: 208). However, it was also a concrete depository of a rich oral culture that almost seemed anachronistic: this incredible store of stories, legends, profiles, motifs radically enriched Sokolov's imagery. The anecdote from which his novel *Between Dog and Wolf* originated derived from the Bezborodovo experience. The anecdote concerns an unresolved and tragic feud

---

[10] His name is indirectly mentioned in Sokolov's second novel (Caramitti 2001: 131).
[11] In this sense, particularly telling are the images of the Russian province found in the works of Valentin Rasputin, Fedor Abramov, Vasily Shukshin, and Chingiz Aitmatov.

between the previous gamekeeper—who was eventually found drowned in the river—and his neighbor.

Bezborodovo and the adjacent villages along the Volga river constitute a highly mythopoeic place in Sokolov's mental map. These landscapes did not disappear from the writer's memories even after emigrating: when later on, in Vienna, at the Kunsthistorisches Museum Sokolov found himself admiring some paintings by Bruegel the Elder,[12] he was surprised to find such strong similarities with the hunting estate where he had lived two years earlier.

In 1982, Sokolov devoted a section of his essay *Na sokrovennykh skryzhaliakh* (On Secret Tablets) to Bezborodovo:

> Strange, mysterious, and tragic events occurred in that indigent place, where, besides me, Chaikovskii, Prishvin, and Rilke with his Russian translator Drozhzhin used to find peace and freedom, but where a man's soul is not worth much more than a pair of boots. There the Volga, otherwise known as the Lethe, flows until it runs into the Turkish sea of oblivion. Enjoying tea made with its water and learning what is going on around its banks, you become forever privy to the inexplicable and unfamiliar—in the river itself and in the fates of those doomed to be with her (2012: 6).

In Bezborodovo Sasha Sokolov had time to observe, listen, create, and write. *Between Dog and Wolf*, which recovers many images and voices 'recorded' by Sokolov during his period spent on the Volga and left to settle over time, would appear only later on.

From this 'retreat', from the poetic forge of the 'gamekeeper' Sokolov, a different text resulted. Yet, *A School for Fools* could not be officially published in the Soviet Union.[13] This book became an unexpected success only after the manuscript reached the publishing house run by Carl and Ellendea Proffer in Ann Arbor, Michigan. *A School for Fools*, published in 1976, was the first book by a debut author for Proffers's Ardis.

---

[12] On the ekphrastic elements that link Sasha Sokolov's oeuvre to Bruegel's paintings, see Johnson 1982, Caramitti 2000, Baknina 2015, Napolitano 2018.

[13] It was not a 'politically' anti-Soviet novel, yet it did not conform to the sanctioned principles of Socialist Realism. As Salomatin and Skvortsov observed, for Sokolov "Soviet literature is not an occasion for confrontation: it should either (more often) be carefully avoided and not touched upon, or (less often) elegantly and succinctly played upon. The position [of this author] is to tacitly ignore the Soviet and continue the classical tradition as if it had never been interrupted" (2021).

Crossing the border, however, was not easy, neither for the novel, nor for its author. The nearly illegible manuscript somehow arrived in the United States via Alexandria, Egypt in very poor condition with no indication of author or provenance (Vail', Genis 1986a: 21). If not for Johanna Steindl, an Austrian lecturer of German whom Sokolov met in Moscow, not only would the text not have reached its perspective publishers, but Sasha Sokolov himself would not have obtained official permission to leave the country.

Getting ready to leave

In 1974 Sokolov's first daughter, Aleksandra, was born. Having returned to Moscow from Bezborodovo, he decided to follow his wife Taisiia to her native Georgievsk (Stavropol krai) in the Caucasus. Here the two worked together for the newspaper "Leninskaia pravda", yet only for a short period, as Sokolov decided to break free from this relationship, leave the family and resettle in Moscow. Until his emigration he worked as a boiler stoker in Tushino, on the outskirts of the city. During this period, he met Johanna, who would embody the possibility for Sokolov to leave the Soviet Union, a desire that the writer had cultivated at least since 1973, when he had tried to cross the border with Iran.

In July 1974, Johanna Steindl began to inquire at the Canadian consulate about the writer's possible expatriation, naively handing over Sokolov's birth certificate registered in Ottawa. The results of this action were not long in coming, and the following day the young man was arrested and interrogated, resulting in the KGB's constant surveillance of Sokolov. Steindl and Sokolov began to do the necessary paperwork to arrange their marriage, opting for the path that seemed bureaucratically easier. As a Soviet citizen, however, in order to marry a foreign woman, Sokolov had to obtain the explicit consent of his parents, who, as loyal members of the Soviet nomenklatura, not only categorically refused, but also raised doubts about their son's mental health, mentioning his convincing simulations of twelve years earlier (if infirmity was not confirmed, Sokolov had to comply with the obligations of military service that he had previously eluded).

In the meantime, by putting pressure on the President of the Supreme Soviet, Nikolai Podgornyi, Sasha and Johanna received a positive response: the wedding was set for June 4, 1975. In spite of this development, Johanna was refused a visa to the Soviet Union since she had returned to Austria in April, so she had to redo the paperwork for a short thirty-day visa that allowed her to arrive in Moscow just in time. On June 4, she was arrested by the police directly at the airport, and the wedding was cancelled. The new date set for the wedding was September 23, but when Johanna's monthly visa expired, she returned to Austria, being immediately branded *persona non grata* by the Soviet authorities: she was no longer granted a visa. In the meantime, however, Sasha and Johanna's love affair reverberated across the world, echoed by major European and American tabloids and newspapers.

On September 4, Sasha Sokolov sent a letter directly to Leonid Brezhnev, in which he wrote:

> I have grown up in a country where the idea of human dignity is instilled from childhood, where the word FREEDOM can be read even in alphabet books, and it is bitter and disgraceful to have to beg someone's grace, someone's permission for something that constitutes a right of any citizen of any state for the simple reason that they belong to the human race. It is bitter and disgraceful, having ascertained one's impotence in front of the faceless and heartless machine of bureaucracy, desperately striving to track down justice within one's borders, to have to call the attention of Western politicians through the foreign press: so that perhaps someone will hear of our misfortune and make the slightest mention of it to someone ABOVE (Mss 117, Box 1: 4).

On September 16, Johanna sent a letter to the United Nations, pointing out that the USSR was not respecting the human rights guaranteed by the Helsinki Accords that the nation signed in the summer of that same year. On September 23, Johanna also went on hunger strike in front of the Soviet embassy in Vienna, an event which was widely reported in the press. The case finally reached the ears of the Austrian Chancellor Bruno Kreisky, who decided to intercede for the couple with the Soviet authorities. On October 8, 1975, Sasha Sokolov, disowned by his family, was allowed to leave the country and moved to Vienna, where he finally married Johanna. In 1983, participating in the conference "The Reevalution of Human Rights" in Florida, the author remembered that moment:

> I quickly threw into my suitcase a few unnecessary things and, without saying goodbye to anyone, executed the latest departure from my repulsive milieu. Since the masses did not justify my hopes, I solved the question of emigration in an individual way. It was my most difficult departure. I think that it succeeded because I was ready to sacrifice for it almost everything. And, essentially, I did sacrifice almost everything (2012: 13).

The manuscript of *A School for Fools*, meanwhile, was already in the hands of the Proffers in the United States, as Johanna managed to take it with her well before the expatriation of her future husband.

A stopover in Vienna

Sasha Sokolov spent less than a year in Austria since his relationship with Johanna quickly deteriorated, and the birth of a son, Daniel, could not convince the writer to reject Carl Proffer's offer to join them in Michigan in September 1976. In Vienna, Sokolov found a job as carpenter, but above all he eagerly immersed himself in books previously forbidden to him in the Soviet Union, beginning with Vladimir Nabokov's novels. The continuous correspondence with the Proffers—a rather unusual mail exchange, as the publishers wrote in English, while the author answered in Russian—was rich in bibliographic requests (reading recommendations and books) from Sasha Sokolov.

An excerpt from *A School for Fools* was first published, for commercial purposes, in the San Francisco Russian-language newspaper "Russkaia zhizn'" on February 20 and 21, 1976. In spring, the book was published in full, receiving positive reviews and garnering support from intellectuals like Vladimir Veidle and Nina Berberova for the young and unknown talent. The first translation into English, by Carl Proffer, appeared almost at the same time (at first some extracts, then the entire novel). In 1977 the book was translated into German, and the year after in Dutch, by Wolfgang Kasack and Gerard Cruys, respectively. Between July 22 and 24, 1977 "Voice of America" broadcast a live reading of some excerpts from the book.[14]

Immediately after the publication of this first novel, both Western and Russian émigré critics[15] did not spare words of admiration: the press defined this new author as the heir to the best world literary tradition, as a voice destined to revive Russian literature. "Who writes like this at the age of thirty cannot but become a

---

[14] In these years the American press published a number of interviews to Sokolov and short articles about him (De Jonge 1976; Jo 1976; Greenberg 1977; Seltzer 1977).

[15] In the Soviet Union critics could officially read and interpret the novel only in the late 1980s. Such delay marked Sokolov's reception in his home country. Since the beginning, it was primarily the American context—refuge for many Russian émigrés—that welcomed the author and studied his oeuvre.

great writer," Vladimir Veidle affirmed (1976: 10). Vladimir Nabokov—unusually for him—celebrated Sokolov's talent, and his words—"an enchanting, tragic, and touching book" (*obaiatel'naia, tragicheskaia i trogatel'neishaia kniga*)[16]—have accompanied *A School for Fools* ever since. Both academics and fellow writers appreciated this first novel by Sokolov, emphasizing different aspects and elements. Representatives of the so-called 'First Wave of emigration' saw in Sasha Sokolov their own heir; those of the 'Third Wave' interpreted the novel as a text dedicated to their generation, steeped in their own experience (Komarova 2013: 85). Halfway between archaism and innovation, Sokolov immediately left a mark on Russian literature, as a representative of his generation and a prophet of a rebirth who combined archaistic and the more innovative tendencies (Matich 1987: 302).

A School for Fools is narrated by the unnamed "student so-and-so" who suffers from split personality and attends special education classes. The narrative is set in a dacha village, located an hour and twenty minutes by train from the city. It is a closed, hermetic, and concentric space, enclosed between the station and the river. The railroad runs all around the village almost as if to strangle it, to suffocate any escapism or centrifugal tendency:[17]

> When one looks at the map of our city, where the river, streets, and highways are marked, it appears that the ring railroad is strangling the city like a steel noose and if, after asking the constrictor's permission, we were to get on the train passing by our house, that freight train would make a full circle and a day later would return to the same place, to the place where we boarded it. The trains that pass our house are moving along a closed—therefore endless—loop around our city and that's why it's virtually impossible to get out of our city (2015: 130).

The boy dreams about escaping from the world of prohibitions and rules in which he is forced to live.[18] He wishes to cross the river and reach the other bank,

---

[16] These words were written by Vladimir Nabokov in a letter addressed to Carl Proffer (May 17, 1976; Mss 117, Box 1: 8).

[17] As critics Pyotr Vail' and Alexander Genis noted, the railway, which in the classic Russian novel serves as a source of encounters and adventures, is here reinterpreted as an impassable boundary (1993: 14).

[18] The boy's father, headmaster Perillo, and Dr. Zauze represent the main forces of constraint; their recurring threat is to send the boy to an undefined other place, where he would be required to undergo coercive treatments of adaptation to social rules.

the shore of imagination, beauty and freedom, where everything is possible, even declaring his idealized love to the botany teacher Veta Arkadievna. The station and the river are the boundaries of this closed world: one is the entrance gate for those coming from the distant and undefined city; the other one is the impassable wall governed by an impervious nature that can only overwhelm man. Both these places have no name; it is simply said that "the station was called," "the river was called" (the "student so-and-so" will then decide to name the river Lethe). These borders are so sacredly impassable that they cannot even be named. Extremely attracted by the river, by the beauty of nature in which he feels he can be transfigured (by the river bank the boy will undergo metamorphosis into a water lily), the "student so-and-so" is aware that this environment is forbidden to him. Sokolov's novel offers no solution and no real conclusion. The narrative—essentially built on a binary structure, which has led D.B. Johnson, in perhaps the most complete commentary on the novel to date, to propose a structural analysis of the text (1980)—aspires, like its main character, to escape the paratextual boundaries of the pages and to cross over into reality, something reminiscent of Daniil Charms's style:[19] "it's time to finish the book: I ran out of paper" (2015: 117).

As his first novel gained international success, the writer began to write a second book: he sent the first drafts to Ardis in the summer of 1976. Sokolov spent these months away from Vienna and, especially, from Johanna, who—according to the letters the writer sent to Proffer—suffered from psychic disorders and depression, worsened by the certainty of her husband's departure for the United States (she did not intend to follow him).

In Switzerland, the writer worked hard on his second novel near Lake Maggiore, and in July, during a train trip between Zurich and Locarno, he also composed the first poem to be included in the book—in the final version, it corresponds to *Zapiska IX—Kak bud'to sol'ju kto...* (Note IX—As if one salted...). In August, Sokolov received a first response from Proffer: he had read the 150-

---

[19] Daniil Charms (Daniil Ivanovich Yuvachev, 1905-1942) was one of the last representatives of the Russian Avant-Garde and a member of the OBERIU (Union of Real Art). He primarily authored short prose—but also transmental poems—moving between the surreal, the absurd and the paradoxical.

page draft and found the text almost incomprehensible. The author thus replied explaining the genesis of the novel, which had already begun in Moscow, and reassuring his publisher about the new direction taken in the writing:

> I just want to explain: I thought up this book as a parody-novel, or as a half-parody. My intention was to make a parody of whatever comes to hand and in sight, as the story unfolds. And I wanted to vary the style. In *Parenthetical Digression*, as you correctly understood, I am parodying Gogol. But I am probably not mature enough for such a book. Or there is another reason: I began to sing in a voice that was not mine. From the very start (Mss 117, Box 1: 5-6).

That month Sasha Sokolov unwillingly participated in the Alpbach Forum dedicated to the freedom of speech in the Soviet Union and in Central and Eastern Europe. In September, thanks to the visa and employment contract provided through Ardis,[20] Sokolov left Europe and landed in the United States.

A North-American nomad

Sokolov arrived in Ann Arbor, Michigan, in the fall of 1976. Carl Proffer had arranged a series of contracts and appointments for him, including lectures and readings delivered at a number of universities in 1977. During a stay at UCLA he met Lilia Parker, who later became his wife from 1978 to 1980. Meanwhile, Sokolov also sought Canadian citizenship, which he received in 1977.

Contrary to other émigré writers, however, Sokolov felt the urge to constantly escape from urban centers, heading towards Vermont, or Quebec—rural and isolated oases, suited to his restless nomadic and solitary spirit. In these years he was constantly on the move, as demonstrated by the many different addresses appearing on the letters he sent to the Proffers. For example, in June 1978, he was in Montreal, a city he appreciated above all for its cultural elite and the local Russian community; in July he was invited to Norwich in Ontario to read extracts from *A School for Fools*; in September he wrote to Carl Proffer of his presence in Los Angeles, while mentioning his next move (or rather, escape) to Quebec. In a letter dated September 26, he acknowledged: "Just now I do begin to realize that

---

[20] The debt owed by many Russian writers to the publisher Carl Proffer (who died of cancer in September 1984) was recognized by several voices on April 1, 1985 at the New York Public Library, during an event in his memory: on this occasion Sokolov read the essay *Otkryv—raspakhnuv—okryliv* (Having Discovered It—Opened It Wide—Given It Wings).

I will never stop changing states, continents, other people's cushions. It is not planned, I cannot stop. That is all" (Mss 117, Box 1: 5-6).

In 1978, despite much travel and public speaking, Sokolov completed the first draft of his second novel, and sent it to Ardis. *Between Dog and Wolf*, however, did not entirely convince Carl Proffer, who on June 28 explained to the writer his own difficulties:

> It was a rather depressing experience, because while I would be the last to boast of my Russian, I did think I understood most things. But I cannot get through a page of the novel without tremendous difficulties. The problem is mostly lexical—I have to look up so many words; when this is combined with the elliptical style of the narration(s), and with your own undirectness of plot and characterization, I am totally lost. I've tried three times, and at different points in the novel, to make progress, but it's hopeless. [...] Needless to say, this is frustrating to me—personally. I was really looking forward to reading your book, and now you're going to have to sit down and read (interpret) it to me (Mss 117, Box 1: 7).

A new version of the novel was ready at the beginning of the following year. The author, now convinced that the book was definitively finished, began to worry about formal and graphic arrangements: in March 1979, Sokolov definitively made up his mind regarding the title, and proposed some ideas for the cover design; in May he announced having found the perfect image (a faded photo of a gamekeeper); in October he worried about the accents with which some words had to be printed for ease of reading and understanding.

However, not even this draft, which was very close to the final version, pleased everyone: in particular, Nina Berberova—to whom Proffer sent the manuscript—expressed deep disappointment in the promising writer's second book. In any case, Proffer had already made up his mind: he blindly trusted Sasha Sokolov and would publish the book anyway the following year. Proffer was even interested in a possible English translation, involving Sokolov's wife Lilia: as the writer explained in a letter dated August 1979, she was working on the "translation of the sense" (*smyslovoi perevod*) of the book, which will then be passed on to UCLA professor Michael Heim for a stylistic rendering. In the end, no translation would appear; Heim gave up, choosing instead to devote himself to the translation of Sokolov's third book, *Palisandriia*, published in Russian in 1985 and in English (titled *Astrophobia*) in 1989. Proffer himself tried to translate *Between Dog and Wolf*—yet with poor results, as he acknowledged on August 7, 1980:

> Virtually at every phrase some explanation is needed. And that still leaves the even more basic problem of whether something which is so rooted in the Russian languages, with all its separate traditions and concepts, its own country life and mind, can have any meaningful equivalent in English. And I surrender. And I surrender not in lack of faith, just in plain helplessness (Mss 117, Box 1: 7).[21]

In the meantime, some positive comments had arrived directly from Moscow. The writer Yevgeny Popov in particular profoundly appreciated Sokolov's second novel:

> Dear Sasha, I have read your new book with joy and pleasure. Your perspective on Russia, on what is called the 'people', is dear and close to me. It is a profound, penetrating glance, so commendably different from the cloying stylizations of Valentin Rasputin, who at the moment in our country is considered almost the champion of the people's spirit—even among intellectual circles. Your glance is at the same time elevated and far from banal stylizers such as Maramzin, on whom, in fact, it is not even worth 'spitting'. In your novel there is tenderness for the country and the people, and for me—a reader tired of the buzz, howls and stabs—this is extremely important and necessary. I wish that you would write (Mss 117, Box 1: 7).

Critics in the Soviet Union (unofficially) showered this second novel with praise, awarding it the 1981 Andrei Bely prize for the best Russian prose. The book had reached the other side of the Atlantic and had been published via samizdat by the magazine "Chasy".

Sokolov's second novel, like its predecessor, belongs to the modernist tradition, as Johnson noted (1984): it is a composite text, built (at least) on three levels, one of which is a poetic cycle authored by a "Binging Hunter", while the more general framework is a stylization of the epistolary novel. Between the two there is the prose of Yakov Palamakhterov, who aspires to become a poet, in whose writing we find many echoes of Russian classics. The fictional author of the long letter that opens and closes the novel is Ilya Petrikeich Zynzyrela, whose name references the mythic and the prophetic alike (e.g. Zynzyrela-Cinderella, Elijah the prophet). However, what can be assumed from the *Zapiska* (Note) *XXVI* is that the entire novel may be but a reconstruction or recollection of different voices and stories sketched down by the "Binging Hunter" only (or rather by

---

[21] An English translation of the novel appeared only recently, in 2017, by Alexander Boguslawski, who previously translated it into Polish in 2000 (*Między psem a wilkiem*). In 1990 a short excerpt appeared in German on the pages of "Schrebheft", translated by Birgit Veit (*Dsyndsyrelas Transitilien*).

Yakov, to the extent we can assume he *is* the author of the *Notes*—and such a first name, so close to the Russian word *iakoby*, makes him literally only 'allegedly' an hunter, a wannabe poet/artist, or, more generally speaking, a round and authentic character). Be that as it may, *Between Dog and Wolf* disrupts—as do all Sasha Sokolov's texts—the idea of the monolithic character, hero and/or narrator, putting forward a concrete example of the natural plurality of voices encountered in any human 'identity'.

The novel can be interpreted, in its own way, as a fairy tale—it is "a complex tale of vengeance and violence" (Johnson 1986a: 639)—set in an apparently distant, archaic, yet incredibly realistic world of territories located by the Volga river. As in fairy tales, the narrative carries a universal meaning that transcends time and space, as Andrei Zorin pointed out (1989: 252).

The story derives from an anecdote. Ilya writes a letter to the investigator Pozhilykh (his ungrammatical language mirrors his being a traveling one-legged knife-grinder from the deep Russian province). Among various Gogol-like digressions, the dynamics of the theft of his crutches and his subsequent death (although the reader becomes aware of this only later in the narrative) unfold. Due to darkness and to alcohol, Ilya in fact mistakes a dog for a wolf and, feeling endangered, engages in a fight with the animal, eventually killing it. This episode triggers a series of reciprocal vendettas, until Ilya is drowned in the river.[22]

Such story concretizes the phraseological expression contained in the title of the novel: as Johnson has highlighted, "between dog and wolf" is not only a thematic key to understanding the twilight atmosphere of the novel, nor is it a simple quotation from Pushkin's *Onegin*. The expression literally implies the inability of the protagonist to distinguish between a dog and a wolf in the twilight. On the symbolic level, it suggests our (in)ability to distinguish between the wild and primordial and the domestic and tamed, the original and the copy, the prototext and its parody—"one must be able to tell the wolf from the dog" (Johnson 1984: 213).

---

[22] After Ilya kills the dog by mistake, a series of acts of vengeance results first in the theft of his crutches—something the reader gets to know at the beginning of the novel—and then in his death. The narrative follows not a circular development, but a spiral model, as the same events constantly reoccur being re-narrated under different guises.

As usual in Sokolov (and in modernist novels), language lies at the heart of the book, even justifying the unfolding of the events. Rather than a fairy tale, *Between Dog and Wolf* is an inversion of the typical fairy-tale structure, a deconstruction, a modernist parody, in which the associations underpinning linguistic expressions subvert and play on the literal meaning. Everything is defamiliarized due to the fact that it has been taken seriously, literally. Metaphors and puns are ready-made metamorphoses. What is promised is constantly betrayed, as Vadim Kreid underlines:

> At the heart of the novel lie all the key elements that could make it an interesting story: adventures, jealousy, revenge, love, murder, eccentricity, and extravagance. However, these possibilities remain all consciously unexploited (1981: 216).

The disruption of the reader's expectations is continuous and starts at the very beginning, with the writing of a letter of complaint by a character we later discover to be dead. In such a world governed by "chaotic chronology" (Johnson 1984: 209), the absence of time (*bezvremen'e*) constitutes an illness, a possibly fatal ailment: "in Russia the main characteristic of time is to resemble *bezvremen'e*," and "*bezvremen'e* is the incurable illness life in the Zaitil'shchina [the mythical setting of the novel] suffers from" (Kreid 1981: 216). However, this fatal defect does not preclude salvation through beauty, which remains, à la Dostoevsky, "the main value of life" even along the Volga river: "whatever happens [...], there is always beauty in life" (Kreid 1981: 216).

Sasha Sokolov, the lecturer

In the meantime, Sokolov continued to work as a lecturer in various universities; in Irvine, California, in the spring of 1979 he met bard Bulat Okudzhava, who was also invited to speak at US colleges that year. The writer spent summer and fall in Montreal, as a speaker for "Radio Canada". In his mind, however, the idea of a third novel was already emerging, a book that, according to him, "would end the novel as a genre" (Johnson 1987a: 217). In support of this goal, Sokolov applied for an Arts Grant offered by the Canada Council in 1981 with the support of the Proffers, but his application was rejected.[23]

---

[23] This is how he described the new project to Carl Proffer in order to apply for the Canadian grant: "I'm now in the process of writing a philosophical, futuristic novel with the elements

During 1980, the writer delivered additional lectures, especially in California (Monterey and Irvine). At this time, Sokolov cultivated friendships with members of the Russian émigré community, such as Aleksei Tsvetkov and Eduard Limonov. Sokolov had also left Lilia for Karin Lundell, a young aspiring interpreter: they now lived together in a small apartment in Pacific Grove, California. In the apartment's claustrophobic restroom, as Johnson attested (1987: 218a), the author wrote much of the future *Palisandriia* (a novel in which the tub indeed plays a big role).

The 1980s were the years of Sasha Sokolov's lectures. The transcripts of his speeches constitute the corpus of his important theoretical-poetic—or rather *proetic*—essays. In May 1981, Sokolov read *On Secret Tablets* at the "Third Wave Conference" organized by Olga Matich at USC; other writers present were Andrei Sinyavsky, Vasily Aksyonov, Vladimir Voinovich, Viktor Nekrasov, Sergei Dovlatov, Yuz Aleshkovsky, Eduard Limonov, Aleksei Tsvetkov; the proceedings were published in 1984 in *The Third Wave: Russian Literature in Emigration*. In March 1983 Sokolov was the only Russian writer to be invited to present at the Cornell Nabokov Festival. After having initially accepted the proposal (to talk about "the influence of Nabokov on his work"), he then decided not to participate. The same happened in April at the conference "Russian Literature Today" at the State University of New York at Stoney Brook. Instead, he attended the conference "The Reevaluation of Human Rights" organized in Florida by Emory University, where he read the essay *V dome poveshennogo* (In the House of the Hanged), dedicated to his experience of emigration.

In the spring of 1983 Sokolov also finished his third novel, *Palisandriia*, which had to wait more than a year and a half to be published. While Carl Proffer was sick and fighting against cancer, the content of the book had literally shocked the publishers. According to the writer, "from me—a definitively lyrical poet, to them—they did not expect that. Sokolov went into politics! That is not good!" (Matveev 2015). However, more than anything else, Carl Proffer seemed to

---

of a political lampoon. The action of it unfolds at the beginning of the 21st century in Russia, Europe, Canada and USA. The size of the novel is expected to amount to 700-80 [sic] type-written pages" (Mss 117, Box 1: 5-6).

disapprove of the style and graphics adopted by Sokolov in the novel. He wrote to him on May 2, 1983:

> My reaction to the CONTENT is as positive as it was after the first page, in spite of the problems of dealing with a piece taken from the middle of a large book. Here I have the same faith in you as always. However, I have to say that I think your purely FORMAL 'inventions' are a disaster. I mean the absence of capital letters and periods, and the use of the 'stroficheskaia' graphic lay-out. You say this is your invention. It isn't. Bely did things very much like this regularly. They didn't add anything to his prose, and they don't add anything to yours. Lots of people have written without punctuation. That seldom adds anything either. No more than Mayakovsky using a 'lesnitsa' line and writing in perfectly normal iambic tetrameter. It's not new. And it's not important. Indeed, it is trivial, and has only one result: annoying the reader, making his job more difficult, destroying the normal process of reading. You are a poet, not a prose writer. But it is silly to think that graphic lay-out makes any difference in this. The true poetry is inherent in the words, the rhythm and the thought. It is there, simply there, simply IS, if you are a poet (Mss 117, Box 1: 7).

All the graphic and formal devices mentioned—the absence of capital letters and punctuation—were indeed eliminated from the final version of the book.

The following year, relations with Ardis worsened temporarily: Sasha Sokolov, in the grip of economic problems, stubbornly accused the Proffers of not having guaranteed him the proceeds from the copies sold; Carl and Ellendea responded coldly to these accusations, clearly stating that "Ardis did not get rich from your books, and does not expect to" (January 22, 1984; Mss 117, Box 1: 7). Relations improved by the spring, and Sokolov even helped the Proffers by proposing some names—such as Nina Voronel' of the magazine "22"—for a literary forum to be held in Ann Arbor.

In December 1984, within the framework of the annual AATSEEL conference, a panel was organized dedicated to "Sasha Sokolov and the Avant-Garde"—the émigré writer Vasily Aksyonov acted as a moderator (in the presence of Sokolov himself). Meanwhile, over the course of the following two years, BBC and "Voice of America" broadcast live radio readings of Sokolov's novels.

Palisandriia was published in April 1985, with its final changes induced by the death of the Soviet leader Andropov, one of the central characters in the novel. As for the formal and graphic aspects, the writer proposed a few alternatives for the cover design, including Melamid and Komar's illustration of the hero Palisandr.

The first copies of the book were presented and sold at the "Russian Writers in Exile" conference organized at USC. Here, Sokolov read the essay *Palisandr—C'est Moi?*. Focused on his role as an author, in this at once poetic and parodic text Sokolov discusses his writing choices, in particular, his intolerance for the plot and the choice to write "without haste." Finally, he addresses the fallacious identification of fiction and reality.

The publication of *Palisandriia*—a fictional autobiography by graphomaniac Palisandr, son and heir of the whole of Russian history and culture, and future leader of the country—was hailed by the critics as Sokolov's new contribution to the postmodern canon (Matich 1986: 417; Matich 1987: 315; Groys 1987: 178; Zholkovsky 1987); according to Johnson, this book is perhaps the first authentic example of the Russian postmodern novel (1989: 163). According to Mario Caramitti, who authored the Italian translation of the novel, Sokolov, a wise dissimulator, seems to have constructed a novel in order to purposely satisfy the tastes of the critics, so that they can find in it all that they have postulated around the cultural paradigm of postmodernism (2019: 415).

In the fall semester of 1985, Sokolov was employed as a lecturer at the University of Santa Barbara, where Professor Donald Barton Johnson had already started to collect articles, drafts, letters, and notes for what was set to become the Sokolov Collection. In fact, the writer had never shown much of an interest in material, physical possessions. At UCSB Sokolov delivered two lectures/essays: *Portret russkogo khudozhnika v Amerike—V ozhidanii Nobelia* (A Portrait of an Artist in America—Waiting for the Nobel) describes the life of the émigré writer, while *Kliuchevoe slovo slovesnosti* (The Key Word of Belles-Lettres) is a proper literary manifesto in which the author elevates the form—the 'how' (*kak*)—above the content—the 'what' (*chto*). A third essay resulted from a lecture at Rollins College in Florida delivered at the beginning of 1986: *The Anxious Pupa* revolves around the role of language for the writer, which simultaneously embodies the ideas of home and prison.

The writer's popularity was so great at the time that in 1987 the *Fond pochitatelei tvorchestva Sashi Sokolova* (Fund of Admirers of the Work of Sasha Sokolov) was established in the United States.

That year Johnson also edited a monographic issue of the journal "Canadian-American Slavic Studies", bringing together the main critics who worked on the oeuvre of this Russian author. This volume, followed in 2006 by another monographic issue of the same journal, constitutes the main body of scholarly work on the writer. As for the nucleus of the most stimulating interpretations concerning Sokolov's work, we can generally distinguish the articles (mostly dating back to the 1980s) authored by those scholars who happened to be closest to Sokolov in relational terms.[24] Indeed, the meta-literary pages of *Palisandr—C'est Moi?*—a text that results from the author's awareness of this atypical interweaving of private life and literary work—are dedicated to these scholars, identified by their initials: OM (Olga Matich), AB (Alexander Boguslawski), DD (D.B. Johnson), AZh (Alexander Zholkovsky), ATs (Aleksei Tsvetkov).

Soviet Union, *toccata and fugue*

In 1988 Tatyana Tolstaya first officially introduced Sasha Sokolov to the Soviet Union. She mentioned the writer in an interview with Aleksandr Shchuplov published in "Knizhnoe obozrenie" (Shchuplov 1988: 4), and then promoted the publication of an excerpt from *A School for Fools* in the magazine "Ogoniok", authoring a short but passionate introduction to it. Sokolov was in Greece that summer,[25] and could not believe his own eyes. The following year the entire novel was published in the magazine "Oktiabr'" accompanied by a commentary by Andrei Bitov (Sokolov was awarded the Oktiabr' prize). In its third issue of 1989, the monthly magazine "Inostrannaia literatura" included an interview with Sokolov among those conducted between the writer Chingiz Aitmatov and famous émigré colleagues, such as Sinyavsky and Aksyonov (Aitmatov 1989: 245-246). The same year *Between Dog and Wolf* was published in the August and September issues of the journal "Volga", with an afterword by Vladimir Potapov. The essay *The Shared Notebook*—written that year during a stay in Yugoslavia—

---

[24] See more on this topic in the next chapter.
[25] Sokolov claims to have written a fourth novel in Greece, allegedly lost in an accidental fire.

was published in the pages of the Soviet magazine "Junost'". While in the United States the translation of *Palisandria*, titled *Astrophobia*, was printed, extracts from the same novel appeared in Yugoslavia in the pages of "Književna reč", and Dubravka Ugrešić translated some excerpts into Croatian for an anthology she edited, *Pljuska u Ruci*. Having been invited to the Soviet Union in order to collect the Oktiabr' prize, as well as to participate in radio, television, and festivals, Sokolov obtained an entry visa and returned to Moscow. He spent less than a year there, accompanied by his current wife Marlene Royle. He soon felt a new urge to leave again:

> When I came to Moscow in 1989, I spent a year constantly changing apartments, hotels, mainly because there were journalists, graphomaniacs who 'bothered' me... they were all for some reason interested in getting in touch with me. My wife and I counted nine different addresses that we changed within a year. We lived and felt like we were being slowly torn apart. You do not belong to yourself anymore. Sure, people's attention is flattering (until then I had no experience of being of interest to anyone), but after a few weeks you can hardly stand up!... Moscow squeezes you, it wears you out, as if you went through a meat grinder. Moscow gives a lot, but it also takes a lot (Slepynin 2007).

After leaving Moscow, Sokolov found refuge in Vermont, marking the beginning of his ongoing tendency to become even more isolated, living apart from the public scene. He followed his wife's professional commitments, moving nomadically between Florida and Canada. In the early 1990s the writer wrote some short reports and sketches for the Russian section of "Radio Canada" that have never been published in print, but were broadcast on the radio.

In the 1990s and 2000s, Israel—home to a vibrant Russophone community—became a new haven for the author: in 2007, he affirmed that "over the last eight years, about four years I have spent in Israel; I went there mainly because of the language" (Slepynin 2007). In Vermont, he became a ski instructor, and spent some summers teaching Russian.

In these years, the first collections of his writing in the form of volumes appeared in the Soviet Union and then Russia: in 1990, Ogoniok-Variant published his first two novels in Moscow; in 1999, Simpozium gathered all his works (essays included) in two volumes, published in St. Petersburg. Since 2006, Azbuka has republished all Sokolov's works, and in 2007 this publishing house printed a separate volume containing only the essays.

In 2011, however, Sokolov unexpectedly authored a new book, *Triptikh* (Triptych), published by Moscow publisher OGI. This book combines under one cover three compositions previously published in the Israeli magazine "Zerkalo". In 2013 OGI started to republish Sokolov's novels too—these versions are all finely accompanied by black-and-white illustrations by the artist Galia Popova. Finally, in 2020, Azbuka decided to publish the Complete Works of Sokolov.

To return to 1996, however, the writer had briefly—literally in a day—returned once again to Moscow in order to collect the Pushkin Prize, which he had been awarded for "purity of style, independence of destiny, synthesis of classical and contemporary prose, development of the Nabokovian tradition through personal linguistic innovations, active contribution to the development of Russian literature" (Vedomosti 1996: 13). On this occasion, Sokolov read the essay *Konspekt* (An Abstract) to the public, which is a virtuosic short text consisting of a single three-page-long sentence that, while pretending to explain why the author has never written theatrical plays, portrays a kind of autobiographical *canovaccio* of his life.

"An eternal student of the globetrotting department"[26]

The result of Sokolov's time spent in Israel and of the relationships he formed there are his most recent publications. Notably, between 2006 and 2010 the writer authored five short texts, which appeared in the Tel Aviv-based Russian magazine "Zerkalo".

The first of these texts is *O drugoi vstreche* (About the Other Encounter), written in order to be read by the journalist Irina Vrubel'-Golubkina in honor of writer Aleksandr Gol'dshtein, a close friend of Sokolov, at the evening event organized in Tel Aviv at the Beit-Leyvik salon on October 26, 2006. *About the Other Encounter* is a structured response to Gol'dshtein's *Ob odnoi vstreche* (About an Encounter), a short text the author included in his *Aspekty dukhovnogo braka* (Aspects of Spiritual Marriage, 2001) pertaining to his first chance meeting with Sokolov and his wife Marlene. Aleksandr Gol'dshtein passed away in July 2006, and Sasha Sokolov decided to answer to his old friend through another essay. This text is not devoid of humor and inside jokes that suggest the tone and

---

[26] This quote comes from Sokolov's essay *An Abstract*.

emotional connection the two shared, yet it also highlights the profound reciprocal admiration they enjoyed in reading each other's literary works:

> Let me share with you my admiration for these texts. I would like to declare them the best examples of this undeniably special kind of belles-lettres that, as I've been suggesting for many years, should be called *proeziia*. They reveal rare merits. For example, the ability to iron out or even reduce to nothing the contradictions between the what and the how. The ability to invalidate, when necessary, the just-mentioned what and to do this while preserving the dynamic equilibrium of the writing. The ability to arrange the narrative space in such a way that the reader won't doubt even for a second that existence is precisely what is happening here and now, on the given page (2012: 76).

About the Other Encounter also ironically self-portrays its author, immortalizing "sincerely yours Sokolov in the gondola—what do you think, one has to maintain one's reputation, one has to measure up: style is the writer himself"—reaching the San Michele island in order to irreverently "recite the text to the old man Iosif" (2012: 77). Sokolov's antipathy for Brodsky is renowned, and we shall assume Gol'dsthein at least supported his friend in this regard.

In the next issue of the same year, the magazine "Zerkalo" published another very short, graphically defamiliarizing contribution by Sasha Sokolov, titled *Duende*.

Саша Соколов

ДУЭНДЕ*

памяти Энкарнасьон Лопес Хульвес
по прозвищу Архентинита,
танцовщицы канте фламенко

¿ A ?

Август 2005 года
Аркос-де-ла-Фронтера
Андалусия

* Из цикла Испанские Опыты

The rather precise reference to the Spanish poet Federico García Lorca—perhaps the greatest singer and theorist of the Duende—is made even more evident in this text by the dedication that opens it at the top right: "to the memory of Encarnación López Júlvez / called la Argentinita / cante flamenco dancer." Moreover, the paratextual information includes a date and, above all, a place, which can only confirm the reference to García Lorca: "August 2005 / Arcos de la Frontera / Andalusia." The inverted question mark enclosing the letter A is yet another Spanish element. Sokolov himself stated that *"Duende* is clearly the result of my passion for Lorca and for Spanish culture in general."[27]

These two texts were followed by the publication, again in "Zerkalo", in 2007, 2009 and 2010, of the three texts that, together, would constitute the above-mentioned *Triptych*: *Rassuzhdenie* (Discourse), *Gazibo* (Gazebo), and *Filornit* (Philornist). For the first time here—if we exclude the poetic cycle included in the

---

[27] Personal communication, email, December 17, 2017. For an analysis of Sokolov's *Duende* see Napolitano 2020b.

novel *Between Dog and Wolf*—Sokolov approached the 'vertical' form, composing verses structured into numbered 'stanzas'.[28]

Although they all present different lengths—*Discourse* is made up of 50 'stanzas', *Gazebo* of 88, and *Philornist* of 99—these three sections are interwoven through a complex texture of recurring expressions, words, themes, motifs and symbols. Offering an insight into his personal 'poetic lab', Sokolov affirms that the process of writing these texts was very fluid:

> I generally start to write without having a plan, but barely with a vague idea or subject in my head. An interesting syntagm or phrase gives rise to a creative drive, then this phrase is developed. In general, it is very important to immediately find the right note, the right intonation. Much has been written and said about this. In *proeziia*, as in poetry or music, you get nowhere without an intonation. *Triptych* was composed gradually, over a long period of time, but not painfully. There was no single big idea. There were some small ones, which appeared in the process of composition—that's how it always happens: ideas, images, words appear as if by themselves, or they don't appear at all. Then you feel like in a waiting room: you are bored, you dream, you find comfort in the little joys of everyday life.[29]

The result of such work, *Triptych*, is an experimental and in many ways hermetic text composed in its entirety by an uninterrupted dialogue between indefinite voices. Lacking a precise characterization that distinguishes them from one another, it is impossible to identify the different voices; they remain undefined voices echoing in a "resonant multi-voiced garden" (II: 82)[30]. Sokolov states that:

> Possibly, we can approach *Triptych* in many different ways: it can be seen as a three-part *proem*, or as a mini-novel, or as an abstract of a novel, or as three plays for several voices.[31]

A *proem* (a *proetic* poem), a novel, a theatrical play—according to Sokolov, many genres may apply to his latest work, which he considered his best: "*Triptych*

---

[28] A choice maybe reminiscent of the numbered verses of the Bible, a constant stylistic model for Sokolov.
[29] Personal communication, email, January 10, 2019.
[30] For an easier bibliographic reference, I opt to quote verses from *Triptych* (Boguslawski's translation, 2012) using Roman numerals (I, II, III) in order to identify the three sections, and Arabic digits to identify the 'stanza'.
[31] Personal communication, email, January 10, 2019.

is the result of years of work. Some pages are, in my opinion, the best I have ever written. Especially *Gazebo*" (Kochetkova 2017).

Indeed, *Triptych*'s 'vertical' form recalls poetry, while its discursive and polyphonic development relates to theater—and there are many explicit allusions to the world of theater in the text. But can this work be defined as a novel—a "mini-novel" or an "abstract of a novel"?

According to Mikhail Bakhtin's canonical definition (1975), the novel is the only unfinished literary genre, the one still in the making. This textual genre is by its very nature an innovative hybrid that breaks every rule from within, shatters expectations and knows no canon. Every great novel, in short, rewrites the genre. Its main characteristics, which distinguish it from other genres, are its multivocality, its pluridiscoursivity and its dialogism, which, as in the case of Dostoevsky's novels, may be taken to the extreme limit of polyphony. The novel welcomes plurality within itself, and it is also for this reason that it flourishes particularly in times of crisis, while it is suffocated if forced within monological visions of the world and of everyday life. If we consider *Triptych* to be a novel, what are its characteristics, or how does it fit into the genre and renew it?

Triptych's indefinite voices refract and echo each other, overlapping and splitting, touching upon a plurality of topics and using different languages, even creating neologisms, with no respect for a certain uniformity of style or register. In addition to Russian, there are (often marked by italics) Italian, Latin, Spanish, Greek, English, German, French, Japanese, Chinese, Polish, Ukrainian-Belarusian, Sanskrit and Slovenian words and expressions; in addition to Cyrillic, Latin and Greek letters are used too.

At the beginning, after an invitation to read the text as a recitative, one of the voices asks whether the "phenomenon of the counterpoint" is appreciated, a phenomenon "understood, / pardon my hegelian leanings, as some, perhaps, / kind of given, as a fact of musical life / and activity, practice and concretism" (I: 3). The counterpoint is, in music, the technique that combines different melodic lines that develop horizontally, as they coexist and overlap (*punctum contra punctum*, "note against note").[32] Mikhail Bakhtin referred precisely to this technique when

---

[32] Counterpoint was employed as early as during the Middle Ages, but reached its maximum development during the Renaissance, between the 15th and 16th centuries. At that time, it

he gave substance to his theory of the polyphonic novel. Upon analyzing Dostoevsky's novels, he noted how a similar multi-voiced architecture found its analogy in the musical counterpoint.[33]

In this sense *Triptych* embodies a polyphony too,[34] as its indefinite voices simultaneously develop different melodies, combining and altering them throughout the text. Only in the third and final section does the voice of the philornist rise above the others, standing out as an individuality, as he sings his own *aria*.[35] Before then, the text flows sinuously from one voice to another, realizing the full potential of polyphony.

Among the many topics touched upon by the voices, there is one main subject that lies at the center of the entire discourse: the creation of beauty—here defined in Russian by the adjective *iziashchnoe* (finesse). This specific topic is developed both in theory (through reflections upon criteria and methods of composition), and in practice (through the very composition). Often masters of style, such as the Mexican poet Octavio Paz (1914-1998) or the lesser-known Italian composer Antonio Scandello (1517-1580), are invited to define their principles of beauty, to which the voices respectfully adhere in their conversing and composing.

Thus, *Triptych* is both the process and the result of the creation of beauty put into practice by the voices, their attempt to compose the *iziashchnoe*. The work is the concrete outcome of the theory of artistic composition. From the opening *Discourse*, passing through an immersion in the multi-voiced *Gazebo*, we reach in the end the *Philornist*'s pseudo-monologue: this fourth 'vertical' novel by Sokolov is structured around a reflection on the creation of beauty that

---

flowered in its most free and imaginative forms. The works of J.S. Bach—in particular *The Art of the Fugue* (1755)—represent the apotheosis of experimentation in this sense: in Bach the choral counterpoint becomes instrumental. The following popularity of the accompanied monody was also reinforced by the success of genres such as the melodrama.

[33] Actually, Bakhtin notes that, before him, the Soviet critic Leonid Grossman, in his article *Dostoevsky khudozhnik* (The Painter Dostoevsky, 1959), had already highlighted the role of the musical counterpoint in Dostoevsky's work.

[34] However, it is clear that the written text can realize 'polyphony' only within certain limits, as it does not allow the synchronized vocalizing of several voices at once.

[35] *Triptych*'s third part consists of an apparently clearer, and more traditional plot. Here, amidst various digressions, the philornist carries on a conversation with a visitor in the museum where he works. Perhaps this is why critic Igor' Gulin, in his negative review of the book, acknowledged that *Philornist* is the best part of Sokolov's last work (2011).

progressively develops it, concretizing its very composition. The conversing voices constitute a sort of frame, a macro-text, within which scenarios are created and made to overlap as a result of such a continuous rhetorical play.

However, Sokolov suggested that the reader interpret *Triptych* either as a "mini-novel," or as an "abstract of a novel"—a term (*abstract*) he previously employed for the title of his 1996 essay, read when he was conferred the Pushkin Prize in Moscow. An abstract is a quick and sketchy annotation, an outline, a synopsis; in this case, we read an abstract of a non-existent novel: this abstract is the 'novel' itself. *Triptych* is therefore a finite incompleteness, an attempt that has become the result of Sokolov's never-ending experimentation and research on the language, the form, the expression, and the genre. In *An Abstract*, Sokolov seemed to somehow anticipate the coming of this last and much unexpected work:

> From time to time I catch [...] some conversations, essentially, conversing voices, and on the basis of their motifs, that is, the motifs of these conversations, I create sketches, about two or three pages long, no more, and those exclusively for myself; there's no need even to talk about any kind of staging them; they are too superficial, insubstantial, which is understandable, since their sources are exactly the same; only once I did catch a conversation that turned into a play worth anything at all; to use language in the style of billboards, it's a play for a certain number of human voices, providing testimony about the fate of someone not very stable, someone vacillating, incline to change places and escape into freedom-loving lyric poetry; isn't he a Gypsy, one would ask; probably, in part, at least in his soul, as is perhaps every real Russian in whose ears this Sokolovian guitar keeps resounding as it did before (2012: 73).

The multi-voiced work to which the writer refers here could be *Triptych*, but also *A School for Fools*, starring its "not very stable," "vacillating" hero; be that as it may, *An Abstract* offers a key to understanding Sokolov's way of proceeding—always in search for an essentially polyphonic and, in part, mimetic *proetic* writing, capable of condensing the possibilities, the richness of the Russian language.

As for the last two decades, Sasha Sokolov has spent them living a nomadic life, moving from Canada to Israel, participating in literature festivals (like the one held in Turin, Italy, 2011), visiting some old friends (like the former *smogist* Vladimir Aleinikov in his Koktebel dacha in the summer of 2007). He seems to have been almost permanently living in Canada for some time now;[36] in Whistler, a village north of Vancouver, British Columbia, the aforementioned 2017 documentary was filmed.

Triptych was not followed by other publications, if we exclude Sokolov's participation in the special issue dedicated to the 90th anniversary of the magazine "Oktiabr'", in 2014. Almost one hundred Russian writers responded to the call of the editorial staff by sending contributions so short that they could be placed inside the palm of a drawn hand: the project was in fact entitled *Rasskaz s ladon'*, literally "a palm-long short story." Sasha Sokolov's text *Ozarenie* (Illumination) is spread over two open palms—the only work of this length included in the issue:

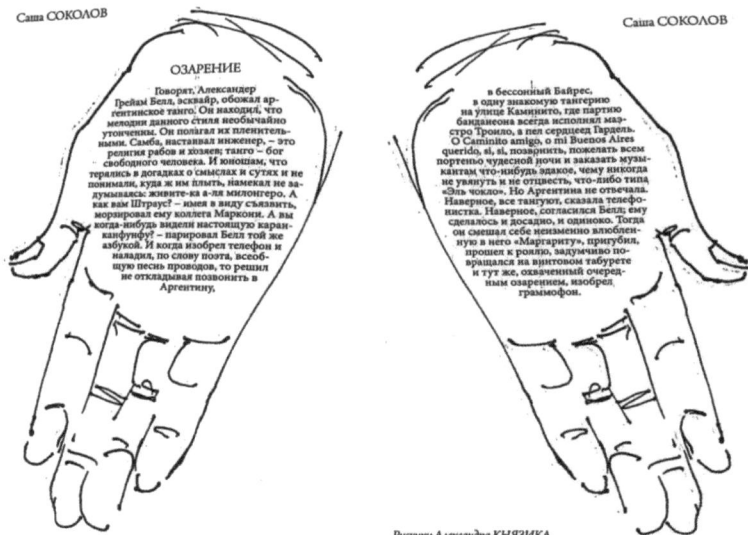

They say Sir Alexander Graham Bell loved the Argentine tango. He considered the melodies of this musical genre to be extremely refined. He thought them bewitching. The samba, the engineer insisted, is the religion of slaves and masters; the tango is the god of the free man. And to young people, who tormented themselves searching for the senses and essences of life, and who did not understand which way to go, he suggested almost without thinking: live like the milongueros. And what do you think of Strauss?, his colleague Marconi communicated in Morse code, intending to be sarcastic. Have you ever

---

[36] The writer affirms that since 2016 he has lived in Montreal (Personal communication, email, July 03, 2019).

seen a real karakanfunfà?[37], replied Bell using the same alphabet. When he invented the telephone and arranged, as the poet [Pablo Neruda] put it, the *canto general* of the wires, he decided with no hesitation to call in Argentina, in Baires [Buenos Aires], in a tanguería he knew on Caminito street, where the maestro [Aníbal Carmelo] Troilo always played a bandoneon piece, and where the heartthrob [Carlos] Gardel sang. *O Caminito amigo, o mi Buenos Aires querido, sí, sí*, call, wishing all porteños a wonderful night, and requesting from the musicians something that does not dry up, that does not fade, something like *El choclo*. Argentina, however, did not pick up. Maybe they are all dancing the tango, said the receptionist. Maybe, Bell asserted; he felt disappointed and alone. So he prepared a faithfully in love with him 'Margarita', brought it to his lips, headed for the piano, thoughtfully rotated on the swivel stool, and just then, caught in yet another illumination, he invented the gramophone (2014: 14-15).

---

[37] A possible neologism from the Polish word *karakan* (beetle) and the German numeral *fünf* (five).

Chapter 2.
On Early Trains, or Beyond Sasha Sokolov's Twilight Cosmos

> "God knows what genre I'll be in by the time we reach Petushki."
> Venedikt Yerofeyev, *From Moscow to Petushki*

As the previous chapter explained, the personality and works of Sasha Sokolov present a fascinating and compelling subject for study and analysis. On the one hand, the author has carefully constructed a certain (masked) image of himself and become part of his own fictional world: Sokolov himself is a 'character' who explicitly strives to maintain such a "reputation," as he states in his essay *About the Other Encounter*; at the same time, the author insists on being different from his characters, as for example in *Palisandr—C'est Moi?*.

This fictional world is characterized by a complex, multilayered texture, which is reflected in the linguistic element that concretizes it. Sokolov's writing is not easily accessible, but it leaves a mark on the reader (and the critic):

> Sokolov is that case in which the vividness, the stylistic expressiveness of the text, the image created by the letters are so powerful that they captivate and overwhelm. Involuntarily, the critic is transformed into Sokolov's shadow, into the mirror image of his texts. Sokolov presents himself as a writing instructor, a profession (considering his work as a ski instructor) that is not entirely foreign to him. It requires a great effort to write about his texts from a certain distance, in one's own voice, without falling into imitation, without involuntarily submitting to Sokolov's manner. As well as to guard against the temptation of excessive quotation. Sokolov is also self-sufficient in quotations (Aleksandrov 2017).

Not surprisingly, Sasha Sokolov has greatly influenced his contemporaries and the generation that followed, in spite of the fact that the Soviet Union officially prohibited his works until the late 1980s (of course, they circulated through samizdat channels). According to the poet Maxim Amelin, "Sokolov's legacy is evident in at least 90% of contemporary Russian literature."[38]

These aspects—the interplay of personal life and literary work, and the multi-layered complexity typical of Sokolov's texts—have had at least two effects on critical approaches and studies: they can be briefly summarized under the terms

---

[38] Personal communication, Moscow, January 7, 2019.

'emotional proximity' and 'classification difficulty'. This chapter addresses these two phenomena, discusses the main interpretations that have emerged so far, and closes by proposing some tools to guide the approach to Sasha Sokolov's complex work.

Emotional proximity

As mentioned in the previous chapter, the publication of Sokolov's third novel in 1985 was accompanied by a short essay bearing a suggestive Flaubertian title: *Palisandr—C'est Moi?*. In this text, the writer reaffirmed his literary credo (the great attention to form, the rejection of the dominance of the plot) and responded with biting irony to those who claim the right to interpret any literary work in the light of its author's biography and personality.

This essay opens with an explicit dedication to five individuals, identified only by their initials: Olga Matich, Alexander Boguslawski, Donald Barton Johnson, Aleksandr Zholkovsky,[39] and Aleksei Tsvetkov. Part of the work of these scholars and, in the case of the latter two, writers, was indeed devoted to Sasha Sokolov. With the exception of Tsvetkov, who has written only one article (the afterword to the 2007 collection of Sokolov's essays),[40] the other four friends of the writer have authored important studies which investigate his work. Aware of this atypical intertwining of private life and work, of friendship and literary analysis, Sokolov devoted his most meta-literary pages to them (those of *Palisandr—C'est Moi?*).

The work of these four scholars dates mostly from the 1980s. Although the 1990s and 2000s have seen an increase in the number of scholars studying Sokolov, the contributions of this original 'friendly circle of critics' remain a fundamental starting point for venturing into the study of the writer's work. Moreover, this group of scholars has periodically continued to enrich scholarship on Sokolov with new and compelling studies.

---

[39] Zholkovsky responded to this essay with *Posviashchaetsia S.* (In dedication to S.), published in "Sintaksis" in 1987.
[40] Sokolov authored a brief preface to the poetic collection *Troe* (The three of them, 1981) by Tsvetkov, Limonov, and Kuzminsky.

Many observations contained in the critical studies published by Johnson, Zholkovsky, Matich, and Boguslawski should be seen as the result of decades of exchanges of ideas and opinions with the writer, who has always been very receptive and inclined to confrontation. As we can apprehend from the letters preserved in the archives of the Sokolov Collection (Mss 117) and among the Johnson Papers (UArch FacP 60), Sokolov is very willing to untangle the opaque knots of his own works in response to criticism.

However, the author usually refuses to engage in further elaboration: the writer's response is often a modest (ironic?) *vam vidnee* ("You see better than I do"), almost as if to distance himself from the critics' acknowledged competence. The interviews Sokolov has given to me in recent years also confirm this tendency to conceal any analytical ability, and to accept with sympathetic ease the interpretative suggestions (as long as they do not concern the name and work of that *redkii merzavets*, "rare rascal," of Iosif Brodsky)[41].

Such an attitude radically distinguishes Sokolov from many other writers who express very harsh feelings towards critics—a well-known example is that of Vladimir Nabokov, who, for example, in *Ada or Ardor* did not hide his contempt for literary criticism:

> Herr Mispel, who liked to air his authors, discerned in *Letters from Terra* the influence of Osberg (Spanish writer of pretentious fairy tales and mystico-allegoric anecdotes, highly esteemed by short-shift thesialists) as well as that of an obscene ancient Arab, expounder of anagrammatic dreams, Ben Sirine, thus transliterated by Captain de Roux, according to Burton in his adaptation of Nefzawi's treatise on the best method of mating with obese or hunchbacked females (*The Perfumed Garden*, Panther edition, p.187, a copy given to ninety-three-year-old Baron Van Veen by his ribald physician Professor Lagosse). His critique ended as follows: "If Mr Voltemand (or Voltimand or Mandalatov) is a psychiatrist, as I think he might be, then I pity his patients, while admiring his talent." Upon being cornered, Gwen, a fat little *fille de joie* (by inclination if not by profession), squealed on one of her new admirers, confessing she had begged him to write that article because she could not bear to see Van's "crooked little smile" at finding his beautifully bound and boxed book so badly neglected. She also swore that Max not only did not know who Voltemand really was, but had not read Van's novel (1971: 270-271).

---

[41] Personal communication, email, July 10, 2019.

In contrast to Nabokov, Sokolov lets the critics do and write as they please; half-playfully and half-mischievously, he seems to enjoy entertaining his interlocutors in their interpretative elaborations.

The willingness to clarify or compensate for certain gaps in the decoding of the texts (e.g. in terms of vocabulary, folklore, hidden quotations) shows us a Sokolov seemingly detached from his own novels: the author acts almost like a consultant called to help critics understand a text that no longer seems to interest him. This lesser-known and obvious aspect of the author's personality, which can be reconstructed from the surviving correspondence, helps to complete the portrait of Sokolov as a 'character', a mask of an author. At the same time, the correspondence and archival materials are useful sources for understanding the extent to which the critics' dealings with the writer influenced their analyses and interpretations.

To give just one brief example, let us focus on a specific correspondence between Sokolov and Johnson[42] concerning the interpretation of *Between Dog and Wolf*. In a letter dated March 3, 1981, the writer explains how to interpret the characters in the novel:

> Yakov Il'ich Alfeev (or: Yakov Olfeev, a biblical episodic character [James, son of Alphaeus]) and Yakov Il'ich Palamakhterov, yes, they are (approximately, because <u>in twilight</u>, Between Dog and Wolf, Inter canem et lupum, everything is more or less <u>approximate</u>, even for me, the author) the same person. The difference in their last names is explained by Ilya Dzinzerela in one of his monologues on family: where are you, Orina (he says), now, where have you gone, "havin taken the son and havin changed your and his last name." [...] Yes, Yakov and Ilya <u>Approximately</u> are son and father, but (although they live close to each other) they do not know it, only the author knows. Speaking with the language of the book, they are possible-father-and-son [otets-i-syn-mozhet-byt'] (UArch FacP 60, Box 12).

In the same letter, responding to Johnson's invitation to explain the fundamentals of Russian folklore ("I don't know anything about Russian folklore and it is obviously important in the novel"; February 24, 1981), Sokolov also points out the folkloric symbolism in the patronymic of the protagonist, Ilya Petrikeevich:

---

[42] Sokolov writes in Russian, while Johnson writes in English.

In Russian fairy tales, the fox has its own patronymic: Petrikeevna. Ilya, if you remember, has the same patronymic, his name is Ilya Petrikeevich. And in the story, he is a little fox, a Fox tied to the tracks. When Orina tells her story, she mentions that from her youth she remembers an episode of a little fox who was killed this way by some "bad people" (UArch FacP 60, Box 12).

In Johnson's essays these clues from the writer are indeed present—for instance:

> Yakov is Ilya's son—to whatever extent anything *is* anything in the twilight world between dog and wolf. Both Yakov and Ilya remain unaware of this, however [...]. These unities [between Yakov, Ilya, Orina, and the mentally defective girl] are established through a fantastic set of murky interconections [sic] involving the fox and the slippers that are bizarrely echoed in both Ilya's patronymic, Petrikeich (the folkloric patronymic of the fox) and in his strange last name, Zynzyrela, with its evocation of Cinderella of vair slipper fame [...]. Alfeev later proves to be identical with the dog keeper Yakov Palamakhterov, with whom he shares his Christian name and patronymic. It is symptomatic of the twilight world that personal and place names exist in alternative forms (Johnson 1984: 211, 217).

Sasha Sokolov's responses to Johnson's inquiries concerning the influence of Nabokov on his literary work turn out to be interesting. Although he often stressed that he had not had the opportunity to read Nabokov's novels until he emigrated, in a couple of letters from 1984 and 1985 Sokolov acknowledged the role of his predecessor on *Palisandriia*: "In the end, the whole novel ideally comes from [*vytekaet*] *Lolita*, being a parody of it" (August 23, 1985; UArch FacP 60, Box 12). In an earlier letter he even declared—with potential irony—to be Nabokov's literary incarnation:

> Considering what you write about the similarity between P. [*Palisandriia*] and Invitation [*to a Beheading*], and considering also what Carl [Proffer] says about the similarity between P. and Ada, in addition to what I see myself—the similarity between many of my images and themes and Nabokov's images and themes in several of our books—one must obviously believe that nature is very generous: she duplicates—for every contingency, as in the case of an epidemic, for example—her artists, in the same generation or in successive, contiguous generations. If Nabokov had not been our contemporary, I would be sure to be his new incarnation, at least the artistic, literary one (May 26, 1984; UArch FacP 60, Box 12).

But Sokolov would also emphasize their fundamental differences, especially the fact that his writing is "driven by an instinctive force. Unlike Nabokov, whom I would describe as a mathematician of literature. Everything in Nabokov is very thought out, schematized" (May 26, 1984; UArch FacP 60, Box 12). Many of Sokolov's responses to this theme appeared in Johnson's article "Sasha Sokolov and Vladimir Nabokov" (1987b).

Access to Sokolov's private letters and exchanges with his 'closest' critics does not permit comments on the quality or originality of these scholarly studies. Nor is the point to show the extent to which a series of studies are 'indebted' to the writer himself. Rather, it is a testimony to the fact that, in order to enter Sokolov's fictional world and comprehend it in its entirety (if one considers it possible), there is definitively an added value in having the author as our personal Virgil, who guides us into its peculiarities. Moreover, interacting with Sasha Sokolov on such a personal level allows the interlocutor to grasp the subtle convergence of styles, tones, images between his narrative and his personal 'idiolect'.

Classification difficulty

> By the way, vagueness as a way of seeing the world and as a method of representing it lies at the foundation of my favourite movement in art and literature. I am talking, of course, about Impressionism (Sokolov 2012: 27).

Always applying syncretic approaches to art, in the essay *The Key Word of Belles-Lettres* Sokolov expressed his preference for Impressionism, which elevated the 'how' above the 'what', and focused all attention on the role of color. If we want to transfer this model to verbal art, then we may be talking about language (the 'how').

D.B. Johnson defined *The Key Word of Belles-Lettres* as a "Manifesto of literary modernism" (1987: 224), a commitment by the writer to a certain kind of aesthetics, reflected especially in Sokolov's first two novels, *A School for Fools* and *Between Dog and Wolf*. The attention paid to form, almost as a polemical substitute for the dominance of linear plot, leads to a reading of Sokolov's work in continuity with the literary tradition of modernism, as suggested by Olga Matich: "Belonging to the modernist tradition, his fiction is verbal rather than ideological" (1986: 416).

However, some critics have expressed doubts about whether Sokolov belongs to the modernist tradition. Indeed, this label is widely used and has become a generic umbrella term, a kind of hypernym applied to any literary work that loosely proposes an epistemological break. Undoubtedly, it is a difficult task to define modernism unambiguously and precisely, given the large and potentially infinite number of different authors who represent this literary tradition. For example, Cynthia Simmons has acknowledged this problem on her part:

> We might classify the literary heritage of the sixties' 'young prose' in the Soviet Union as resurgent modernism. The latter term is employed here in a general sense and encompasses the aesthetic movement—Modernism (dated anywhere from 1890 to 1950)—as well as the formal and thematic strains that have persisted into the post-modern period and constitute the 'raw material' of our twentieth-century aesthetic (1993: 4).

The complexities inherent to the term 'modernism' have also affected the interpretation of Sokolov's work: Russian scholars in particular have proposed a variety of labels (including the 'fashionable' label of postmodernism) in an attempt to classify Sokolov's elusive and unconventional literary output. Indeed, the resurgence of Russian modernism in the second half of the twentieth century has long defied attempts at definition: this literature, at once heir to and distinct from the historical Avant-Garde, presented itself as a "new Russian Avant-Garde" (Johnson 1989); although it lacked the programmatic ambitions and compactness of schools and movements, this new Avant-Garde laid the groundwork for a rebirth of Russian literature that had become stagnant through decades of censorship and socialist realism. As Andrei Zorin wrote after Sokolov's first official publication in the USSR, this writer (along with others) "succeeded in stirring the wind over Russian prose" (1989: 253).

The result of such 'classification difficulty' has created a kind of historical-geographical divide between Russian critics and their Western counterparts. As mentioned above, Sokolov's work did not officially circulate in the Soviet Union until the late 1980s, and this delay strongly conditioned the Russian critics' approach to the study of his novels. The gap catapulted this writer of the 1970s and 1980s not only into a different temporal context, but also into an entirely new social, political, and artistic framework. The post-Soviet climate and, above all, the influence (or 'fashion') of postmodernism and its artistic-cultural paradigm inevitably determined the reception of the three novels of the 'old-new' writer Sokolov in the following decade. Thus, while Western critics associated his first two novels with a resurgent form of modernism, a number of Russian critics—aptly defined by Italian Slavist Donatella Possamai as "postmodernized critics"

(2004: 119)[43]—more often chose the term 'postmodernism' to describe the totality of Sokolov's texts. Only in the case of *Palisandriia* did the two factions agree.

In short, Western critics aligned the young writer with the tradition that—from Gogol to Bely to Nabokov (at the time)—researched the form and sound of language. In interviews, Sokolov himself acknowledged the influence of Gogol on his work, but even more than Bely and Nabokov, he emphasized the influence of Lev Tolstoy and Ivan Bunin, whom he called, perhaps provocatively, "modernist" writers (Matich 1985a: 12). In this sense, the observation first made by Helen von Ssachno and Philipp Felix Ingold in 1979, and further elaborated by Richard Borden a decade later, concerning the proximity and influence of Valentin Kataev, Bunin's student, on Sokolov, was particularly timely. As Borden further recalled, "when at a public forum in 1984 Sokolov was asked which contemporary Soviet writers he had read, he was able to come up with only one name—that of Valentin Kataev" (1987: 249). Apart from Sokolov's unique approach to language, Western critics also stressed that the structure of his first two novels, the nature of the characters, and the associative process at work in these narratives were all related to the modernist sensibility.

As for Russian critics, even before the 1990s many had highlighted the fact that the prose of Sasha Sokolov and other writers of his generation presented a particular problem of 'otherness' that made these authors difficult to categorize even within the broad realm of modernism or the late Avant-Garde. At that time, the new category of postmodernism, which was to explode as an interpretative tool in Russia shortly thereafter,[44] had not yet become commonplace. However, there was talk of a generic 'new prose' and related terminology. Thus, in 1985, for example, Mikhail Berg hypothesized that a new genre had emerged that belonged to what he defined as "vertical literature": it was the "genre of play" (*igrovoi zhanr*), which originated from the experience of OBERIU and absurdist literature.

---

[43] In this article, Professor Possamai maintains that in many cases "the term [postmodernism] in Russia has been applied retroactively" (2004: 118).

[44] This, of course, does not apply to Russian émigré critics who have used the term 'postmodernism' since the second half of the 1980s, such as Boris Groys (1987) in reference to Sokolov's *Palisandriia*.

The reader is astonished to find that the author is most likely mocking at what has always seemed reasonable and sacred to him. The literature of the play tears apart tradition, and more importantly it disrupts the traditional bond with the reader. Traditional literature is a heart-to-heart conversation, and the reader has always felt like a confidant of the writer. [...] The literature of the play no longer gives the reader a chance to feel that way, for the distance between the hero and the reader widens before the eyes like a jackknife. The reader, raising his eyebrows in amazement, suddenly understands that the writer is not laughing at the wounds of reality and the naivety of man, but at him. [...] The reader stands as he were behind the author's shoulders and observes him from there (1985: 5).

A few years later, in response to the need for systematization typical of this confused historical moment in Russia, Oleg Dark counted contemporary writers such as Aksyonov, Venedikt and Viktor Yerofeyev, Dovlatov, Kharitonov, Limonov, Popov, Mamleev, and Narbikova among the representatives of a generic "new prose" (*novaia proza*), "other prose" (*drugaia proza*), "new wave prose" (*proza novoi volny*) (Dark 1990; Dark 1992). Dark interpreted Sokolov's texts as a "guide to this new literature" (1992: 224). Like Berg, Dark perceived this artistic tendency as a tearing apart of the traditional intimate relationship between the author and the reader.

However, it was during these crucial years that the brand-new term 'postmodernism', or more precisely 'proto-postmodernism', was first used in Russian criticism: in 1989 in the pages of "Novy mir" Andrei Zorin made use of it, referring to Yerofeyev's *From Moscow to Petushki*. From then on, critics quickly moved to associate this label with a whole generation of writers: thus, in Russian criticism, Venedikt Yerofeyev, Andrei Bitov, Sasha Sokolov and Andrei Sinyavsky became—not without disagreement—the unconscious progenitors of Russian postmodernism, being placed at the origins of this artistic trend in the well-known history of literature texts authored by Irina Skoropanova (1999), Viacheslav Kuritsyn (2000), and Mark Lipovetsky[45] (Leiderman, Lipovetsky 2003). Mikhail Berg himself, who in 1985 had spoken of a generic new Avant-

---

[45] While Mark Lipovetsky used the term 'postmodernism' loosely in many works dating back to the late 1990s, talking about a wide range of Russian authors (1995; 1997), he later restructured his own notion of 'Russian postmodernism' and divided it into two main directions: Conceptualism and Neo-Baroque. Conceptualism is close to historical Avant-Garde, while Neo-Baroque is a new manifestation of 'high modernism'. Yerofeyev's *From Moscow to Petushki* connects these two currents (Leiderman, Lipovetsky 2003: 425).

Garde with OBERIU qualities, defined Sasha Sokolov's novels as examples of postmodern prose in 1993 (Berg 1993).

Just as the term 'modernism' is difficult to define and apply, so too does the label 'postmodernism' fall short. Not only has its misuse robbed it of specific and stable characteristics but given the cultural divide between the socialist and capitalist worlds in the second half of the twentieth century, it is difficult to apply it equally to artistic artifacts produced in the respective blocs. As the Italian Slavist Mario Caramitti convincingly argued,

> to consider the latter [Venedikt Yerofeyev, Andrei Sinyavsky, and Sasha Sokolov] as proto-postmodernists is, in short, a historiographical hypothesis that is not entirely unfounded but seems very disrespectful—not only in terms of their historical place in a closed system [the Soviet Union] in which authentic literary activity was confined to a dimension that was little more than private, but also in terms of the peculiarities of that system, unprecedented peculiarities in terms of shocking, phantasmagoric means of self-destruction. In the Soviet era, the notion of 'virtual' could have no citizenship [...]. What postmodernism calls 'virtual' is always and only potentially true in the Soviet world (2001: 24).

Since there is no agreement on the meaning and definition of these labels, any application merely underlines their indeterminacy and possible emptiness, which in turn means that the work of Sasha Sokolov defies similar classifications.

Close reading attempts

Given the futility of the search for an appropriate label for Sasha Sokolov's work, insightful studies of his novels have appeared that seek interpretative keys hidden in the narrative itself—an approach reminiscent of the Formalist school, of New Criticism, but also of Yuri Lotman's semiotic studies applied to the literary text (e.g. his interpretation of Pushkin's *Eugene Onegin* through the notion of 'contradiction'). Such an approach to the study of the text does not apply concepts and tools derived from other disciplines,[46] but carries out a rigorous textual analysis, highlighting the recurring features and the 'dominant' that stands out in

---

[46] Although fascinating, these studies may prove invalid or questionable. In the case of Sokolov's work, Barbara Heldt's study of *female skaz* in *Between Dog and Wolf* can serve as an example (1987).

a careful reading.[47] In this way, we may grasp the authors' own theory of literary creation, the genre and style they have carved out for their own literature. The general labels pertaining to genre and style—'modernist', 'postmodern', 'avant-garde'—are secondary.

A proposal put forward by D.B. Johnson in 1986 schematically summarized Sasha Sokolov's "major themes and motifs": through this framework, the critic discerned what he defined as "Sasha Sokolov's Twilight Cosmos," a kind of thematic cosmology that orders the writer's seemingly indeterminate fictional world. Twilight (*sumerki* in Russian) is not simply a recurring word and setting in his novels, but it constitutes an authentic 'chronotope'.[48] According to Johnson's interpretation, four main constellations define Sokolov's narratives: time, memory, sex, and death. The first two are connected to each other by water imagery (usually a river),[49] while the other two by trains and railways. Finally, sex and death are symbolically embodied by the female figure usually called "that

---

[47] "The dominant may be defined as the focusing component of a work of art: it rules, determines, and transforms the remaining components. It is the dominant which guarantees the integrity of the structure" (Jakobson 1990: 41).

[48] Johnson observed that in Sasha Sokolov's works there is a kind of general erosion of the boundaries between opposites: life and death are confused, male and female merge in hermaphroditism (but also in the writer's *nom de plume*, Sasha, as Mario Caramitti later observed (2006)). It is a 'thematic' erosion: "Although our basic coordinates of consciousness are dislocated in all of the works, each novel foregrounds a particular theme: *A School for Fools* is told by a schizophrenic who does not believe in linear time; *Between Dog and Wolf* is narrated by a murdered man in a world where the living and the dead are indistinguishable; the incestuous narrator of *The Epic of Palisandriia* is both male and female. The fixed reference points of existence are destabilized; the boundaries are erased, and we are in the twilight zone" (Johnson 1986a: 649). This "twilight zone" is, according to Johnson's analysis, at the same time the setting, the theme and the metaphor that pervades every dimension of Sokolov's fiction (1989: 168). Before Johnson, Evgeny Ternovsky in 1980 had already advanced the hypothesis that Sokolov's prose revolved around the *sumerki*, the twilight, not so much understood as a moment of the day, but as the literary concretization of indeterminacy (1980: 13).

[49] The Itil' river (the Volga) lies at the geographical center of the world 'between the dog and the wolf'. Its waters separate the living from the dead, though this separation between the two worlds is tenuous, especially in wintertime (Johnson 1982: 169). Moreover, in all of Sokolov's novels we encounter the Lethe, the river of memory and oblivion, which often becomes the border between life and death: "Sokolov fuses the waters of the Lethe and the Styx" (Johnson 1986a: 646). Mark Lipovetsky has also observed that the Volga is identified in Russian culture and folklore as "the River of Life" (1999: 145).

dame" (*ta dama*), or "that woman" (*ta zhenshchina*)—the fatal and attractive "death's handmaiden" (Johnson 1986a: 645),[50] more recently discussed in detail by Italian Slavist Mario Caramitti (2004b).[51]

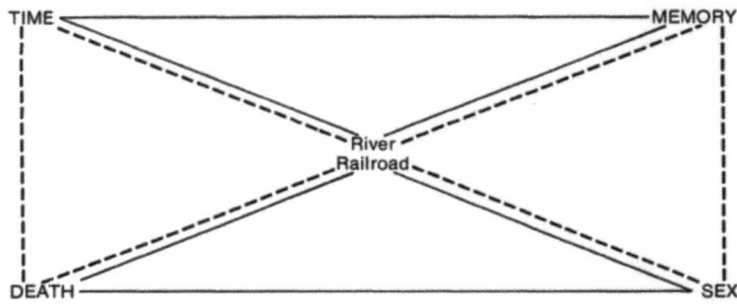

SOKOLOV'S MAJOR THEMES AND MOTIFS

---

[50] Death is also associated with the image of the abyss that devours and kills, by extension a fascinating and fatal return to the womb: "Gaping openings—shafts, keyholes, wells, and spiral stairwells (all *svalina* in Russian)—have obvious sexual meaning in *Palisandrija*. The central image of this complex is the vagina itself as in the following description of Viktorija Brezneva's genitals: 'влажно, смугло и молча гласило ее междометие: О' (*moistly, darkly, her interjection yawned-breathed-and silently proclaimed: O*). The 'O'-image is also associated with Šagane. Palisandr tries to prolong the darkness of his ecstatic first night with her by 'firmly shuttering the cell's embrasure, which had the indecent form of an oval'. 'O' is the emblem of *Palisandrija*'s international feminist movement, and it is not by chance that Palisandr and Šagane's first night of passion is 8 March, International Women's Day. The sexual icon 'O' is explicitly identified with the above death motifs in a second O-saturated passage, in which Palisandr at last confronts his image in the mirror: 'Тогда—зазияло овально. Тогда—засквозило глубокой голубизною осеннего омута—провалом винтового лестничного пролета—о, о—тогда' (*Then-it began to gape ovally. Then with the deep blueness of an autumnal whirlpool it began to show through—like the funnel of a spiral stairwell—o, o—then*). Both the foregrounding of the O-icons and the similarity of language in the two passages affirm the death-sex parallel" (Johnson 1986b: 396).

[51] Caramitti has made some intriguing suggestions about these ambiguous figures. In his interpretation, the figure of *ta dama* is an "all-encompassing poly-character" who appears in three variants or "hypostases": the first is that of "a mysterious woman [who] carries a dark sexual threat and/or temptation"; the second is "a woman who seems more tangible and easily identifiable, [who] is the main object of desire for the protagonist"; the third is "an often mentally retarded young woman, often a victim of violence, who is surrounded by a somewhat more sublimated erotic sphere" (2004b: 114). As for the male characters, Caramitti observed that they yearn to merge with the aquatic element.

Moreover, Johnson observed that a recurring Oedipal theme unites all three novels. In *A School for Fools*, the "student so-and-so" is obsessively jealous of his mother. In *Between Dog and Wolf*, all the characters, both male and female, are multiplied in a series of different "hypostases" (Caramitti's definition (2004b: 114)), bearing different—"Protean" (Johnson 1986a: 648)—names and characteristics, and occurring in different temporal dimensions, but always maintaining an incestuous relationship: Yakov, jealous of his mother ('reincarnated' in a girl suffering from a mental disorder),[52] eventually kills Ilya, unaware that he is his father. Finally, *Palisandriia*, revolves around the motif of incestuous sexual violence, which the protagonist relives through déjà vu and projections into the future. In this sense, incest in the end cancels out any movement in time: incest is that original sin that characterizes, in particular, Palisandr's human experience "in all possible pasts, presents, and futures" (Johnson 1986a: 644). As for the "Twilight Cosmos" scheme proposed by Johnson, the Oedipal plot reveals the interconnections between the four thematic constellations of sex, death, time, and memory.

Alongside this schematic summary of Sokolov's main thematic cores, some 'structural'[53] approaches to the study of his novels have appeared, with the aim of explaining 'how they are made' (to recall obliquely Boris Eikhenbaum's fundamental study of Gogol's *Overcoat*). Without delving too much into the various analyses proposed by critics so far, this section will trace the main findings put forward by the aforementioned 'emotionally closed circle' of critics. These studies contain comprehensive and stimulating insights into the three novels and serve as a starting point for further analysis. Finally, given the lack of scholarly attention that Sokolov's last book, *Triptych*, has received, new

---

[52] Johnson also observed that "one of the most striking 'universal' themes is deformity—mental or physical. Sokolov's heroes—the boy Fool, Il'ia the grinder, and Palisandr the hermaphrodite—are all misshapen. So are many of the women, such as Trakhtenberg-Tinbergen with her artificial limb, the defective girl shared by Il'ia and Iakov, and the legless Shagane, Palisandr's beloved" (1986a: 648).

[53] The use of the adjective 'structural' (here to be understood as loosely referring to those Structuralist theories that would look for the 'structure' inherent in the text) goes back to Johnson's 1980 study dedicated to *A School for Fools*, which he titled "A Structural Analysis."

interpretive tools will be provided to situate this text and examine its structure and main themes.

A School for Fools—A binary novel

As Johnson noted in what is still perhaps the most comprehensive commentary on the novel, *A School for Fools* is built on a binary framework (1980). Johnson's structural reading highlights the mirrored architecture that distinguishes the themes, symbols, objects, actions, and even the names of the characters in this "paradigmatic" novel:[54]

> The theme of the book resides in its fundamental opposition Irrationality/Rationality with the former being the positively defined or marked member. This most basic dichotomy is manifested through three parallel, superimposed, but scarcely less central, polarities: Madness/Sanity, Freedom/Bondage, and Nature/Institutions (1980: 208).

The characters in this novel are dissected, disorganized, split. In Johnson's interpretation, this "ontological polyphony," as Mark Lipovetsky later defined it (1999: 85), reflects the modernist binary structure of the novel: "All of the narrative's major characters are internally paired, that is, they have alternate names and/or identities" (1980: 220).[55]

Between Dog and Wolf—A spiral network of threads

Alexander Boguslawski's article "How Sokolov's *Mezhdu sobakoi i volkom* is made" explores the various threads woven into the complex texture of Sokolov's second novel.[56]

---

[54] Johnson explained that, whereas in a realist novel the reader finds an explicit syntagmatic axis and has to reconstruct the paradigmatic one for himself, here the opposite happens—and this leads to a much less comfortable reading (1980: 233).

[55] In addition to the narrator, who not only feels doubled, but also undergoes a metamorphosis into a water lily, the geography professor is both Pavel *and* Saul Norvegov, the vice-principal and neighbor is both Trakhtenberg *and* Tinbergen, the postman's last name is both Mikheev *and* Medvedev.

[56] The notes that accompany Boguslawski's English translation of the novel are also an important source. In this appendix, Boguslawski conveys the richness of meaning and musical harmony present in the original. The translation process and the constant exchanges with the writer certainly helped Boguslawski in his analysis. In particular, Sokolov's lexical choices concerning temporal categories and the motif of death may have provided an

As in poetry, recurring images in this novel "play the role of the background threads (weft) for Sokolov's word weaving and hold the tapestry together" (2006: 210). The text, extremely precise and studied in its architectural composition, is built on a network of iterated images (dog and wolf, the grinder's craft and his tools, Ilya's crutches, the prophet Elijah, ekphrastic quotations from Bruegel's paintings). In addition to images, phraseological and idiomatic expressions, as well as repetition with minimal variation hold the text together: after all, "Sokolov is a master in synonyms and alterations" (2006: 210).

Intertextuality also builds spiraling inferences into the narrative. For example, in this text (in which nothing is accidental), the 18 chapters and 37 poetic compositions could refer to Pushkin's date of death, 1837 (2006: 207). As for intertextuality, Boris Ostanin's recently published *Glossary* to this Sokolov's novel (2020) is a very useful resource. Thanks to a carefully compiled list of direct and oblique references encountered in Sokolov's text, Ostanin's glossary highlights not only the importance that Russian classics acquire in organizing the narrative, but also the role of popular songs, proverbs, idiomatic phraseologisms, nursery and counting rhymes. The intertextual play in the book draws on literary sources from both high and low culture.

Furthermore, it is worth noting that the complex texture of Sokolov's second novel has also been addressed in a monographic issue of "Canadian-American Slavic Studies" published in 2021, to which an international team of '*sokolovedy*' (Sokolov's scholars) contributed.[57]

Palisandriia—A bricolage of different sources

Alexander Zholkovsky's contribution to the 1987 issue of "Canadian-American Slavic Studies" focused on what he called the "stylistic roots" of Sokolov's third novel.[58] In a meta-literary text like *Palisandriia*, he argues, it is difficult to discern where the line is drawn between intertextuality and the author's style, which is in

---

effective key to the writer's work, leading to an illuminating study published in 1987 ("Death in the Works of Sasha Sokolov").

[57] I co-edited this issue in collaboration with José Vergara.

[58] In a letter to Sokolov dated July 5, 1988, Johnson announced with relief the closure of the journal, which he edited. The scholar is severe and frank about the contributions that were included: in his opinion, "only Zholkovsky is outstanding" (UArch FacP 60, Box 12).

its own way an echo of past traditions. Sokolov inserted explicit quotations and allusions into the novel, creating a "bricolage of different sources" that Zholkovsky managed to list with precision, yet openly admitting the possibility of error. In some cases, it is a matter of "recurrent references" that, taken together, form intertextual "clusters"—such as those concerning the work of Pasternak or Limonov. In other cases, they are "typological parallels"—as, for example, with respect to Olesha and Nabokov ("Olesha and Nabokov are among Sokolov's natural precursors, if not direct sources," according to the critic).

Zholkovsky's analysis focuses in particular on one of the most important intertextual elements that structure the entire novel: the "military and patriotic tradition," often combined with "decadent" tones that are usually diametrically opposed to this tradition.[59] Heir to a formalist and structuralist education, Zholkovsky employs the concept of dominant—ideological, stylistic, and intertextual: "*Palisandriia*'s dominant can be defined as a post-modernist repudiation of the ideological partisanship of the Soviet era in favor of an all-inclusive aestheticism." In this sense, he interprets the military-heroic-epic Russian and European literature as one of the crucial intertextual sources in the novel (beginning with its Homeric title). Zholkovsky divides this intertextual component into subgroups—"referential (or 'real-life'), referential-stylistic, stylistic proper, and linguistic."

In his detailed final commentary, Zholkovsky summarizes perhaps the most interesting aspect of this intertextual novel:

> *Palisandriia* is a forbiddingly 'ethnic' text, making extreme demands on the reader's familiarity with the Russian language, literary tradition, and everyday culture. [...] Sokolov plays mostly with well-known—schoolbench or topical—literary cliches (1987).

Sokolov intentionally designed his *Palisandriia* as an intertextual text intended for a 'model reader' who belongs to the general Russian audience, according to Zholkovsky. The author intended the book to "end the novel as a genre," which it accomplishes by collecting traces of all the various lineages of the European and Russian novelistic tradition. The result, however, is a novel that

---

[59] In a footnote, Zholkovsky also mentions Sokolov's 'military' biography, being the son of a Soviet officer and having attended the Military Institute of Foreign Languages in Moscow.

is complex and difficult to unravel, especially because of its formal aspects. The kaleidoscopic sum of these diverse and often familiar (to the Russian reader) sources has produced a 'non reader-friendly' text. Zholkovsky's observation is particularly true not only for *Palisandriia*, but also for the author's global oeuvre, his recent *Triptych* included.

For her part, Olga Matich took Bakhtin's theory and terminology as a starting point (a choice that also provoked some criticism)[60] and situated the novel's core within a particular process of "Dionysian carnivalization" that revolves around its protagonist. In Palisandr's epic, as in the character of Palisandr himself, we find an inseparable mixture of high and low elements, of tragic and comic tones, of eros and death, of the sublime and the horrific, of youth and old age. According to Matich, the plot of *Palisandriia* is wrapped in two lines of composition: on the one side is the mythical journey of the hero (separation-initiation-return), on the other, the blasphemous adventure of a novel Draculinian-Dionysian Don Juan suffering from a chronic Oedipal complex (1985b: 89).

Triptych—A performative reflection on finesse

Until their publication under one cover in 2011, the three sections (published separately in "Zerkalo") that make up Sokolov's last 'novel' went unnoticed by critics. In 2011, some reviews and articles began to appear: the first two, however, were negative in tone.

Maya Kucherskaya, author of the review published that year by "Vedomosti", avoided proposing any interpretation of the book, as this, she claimed, would lead to "an extremely cold and rational occupation." Although she praised Sokolov's mastery in handling and reactivating the Russian language,[61] her conclusion was a criticism:

> The desire to go on, to continue one's experiment is typical of the honest artist, who has every reason to do so. But the reader also has his reasons. The experiment can be of any content and boldness, but it must be able to pierce the reader's heart from side to side. *Triptych* does not succeed in this (2011).

---

[60] See Viktor Perel'man's harsh criticism of her approach (1986).
[61] For his last book the author created a "linguistic herbarium, a linguistic utopia, demonstrating how the Russian language was, must be and will always remain" (Kucherskaya 2011).

Even more critical and severe was the review of Igor Gulin, published the same year by "colta.ru". In his opinion, *Triptych* is a "book that does not want to be read," because it "fails to meet the reader." Rather, he says, it is a "continuation of [Sokolov's] silence" (2011).

The following year, "NLO" published the commentary of Valery Kislov, which struck a very different chord. In a very concise manner, the critic and translator undertook a preliminary decoding of some of the motifs contained in *Triptych*. Moreover, he placed this last publication in the context of Sokolov's literary production, by pointing out how, for example, the question of time, the motifs of death and metamorphosis were already present in *A School for Fools*. Kislov noted that the apparent absence of an object of discourse in *Triptych* is justified: the object becomes the exposition of the discourse itself, the mode of exposition, the "how" (*kak*), which basically replaces the "what" (*chto*). The critic concluded by saying that with this work Sokolov had reached a new stage in his research on language, understood as an "artifice of liberation" (*priyom osvobozhdeniia*) (2012).

That same year "Znamia" published a review by Vladimir Cherednichenko, who describes *Triptych* as a "more than serious text: there are overtones of thought that are better understood on a second reading." The reviewer noted that in this book, reality is only an illusion, highlighting the importance that the countless lists assume in concretizing this universe of simulacra (2012).

Recently, "Znamia" published another commentary, authored by the writer and poet Gennady Katsov—an ardent reader of Sokolov's work, rather than a critic. Examining the whole of Sokolov's production, as well as his biography, Katsov finally comes to *Triptych*: "What if *Triptych* were a booklet, certainly made of puzzles, like a sudoku, of phonematic charades, of visual rebuses, and it were not meant for the eye, but for the ear, the throat, and the nose?" (2017). In a single question, Katsov outlined the idea (or intuition) that a musical and visual reading of Sasha Sokolov's last work is indeed possible—something that is further explored in the next chapter.

In addition to these reviews, a number of studies have been published in scholarly and academic journals in recent years. Between 2012 and 2013, Mikhail Egorov devoted three articles (published in "Iaroslavskii pedagogicheskii vestnik") to the three sections of *Triptych*, addressing the meta-textual aspect of *Discourse*, the indeterminacy of *Gazebo* and the "narcissistic" narrative in *Philornist*. Yuri Shatin in "Kritika i semiotika" observed how rhetorical devices are mixed with poetic artifices in this book, and how "actively borrowing classical tropes and rhetorical figures, Sasha Sokolov transforms them into building material for a new poetics" (2013: 207).

Especially when compared to Sokolov's three previous novels, the 'critical landscape' surrounding the writer's last work is extremely limited. *Triptych* has passed virtually unnoticed, save for a few reviews, a few articles and an embarrassed silence—which the next paragraphs will attempt to break.

Discourse

Triptych's first part, *Discourse,* is a kind of programmatic and philosophical introduction starring an indefinite number of voices, who prepare, discuss and arrange the discourse itself. The conversation begins *in medias res*: as in the case of *A School for Fools*, the reader is presented with a dialogue that seems to have already begun, and which—due to the brevity of the lexemes and the alliterative repetition—immediately suggests a musical interpretation. The voices mention a list but leave its elements vague, merely repeating the use of the indefinite pronoun *to-to* ("this and that").

The overt musicality of the first stanza draws the conversation into musical and dance-related themes (the counterpoint, the quadrille) (I: 3-4): "all this music, / that is, the conversation" takes place in such an "*amabile*" manner, it is said, that everything external to it, interlocutors included, "don't add up to be important" (I: 6). Indeed, here as elsewhere in *Triptych*, the voices remain undefined: they are mere vocal instruments used to flesh out the music of the speech. Even when one voice emphasizes the passionate way of speaking of the other (I: 5), the latter does not assert its own individuality, but simply states that it follows the example set by Octavio—referencing the Mexican Nobel Prize winner Octavio Paz, a poet and master of the written word who was very attentive to the act of naming and its power.

"There are quite a few" voices involved in the conversation (I: 8) and they are all engaged in the act of composing a "genuine human document," no "literary tinsel" (I: 10). This "human document" is, in the end, the same list mentioned in the first stanza, the precise and at the same time vague list of *to-to*. In it, "any number of things, whether / objects, phenomena, or living creatures" must be collected and enumerated with precision (I: 27): this is the voices' task. This is how true arithmeticians behave, unlike "those / linnaeuses who, for insects and birds, / just because they have wings, / the latter always and the first often, / [find] a common denominator, / [find] a single register" (I: 41). This is the essential message of *Discourse*: "counting is counting" (I: 29), a 'rule' that is cyclically emphasized throughout the work.

The importance of such precise enumeration does not stem from the fact that every object and creature is *a priori* accorded equal dignity. It lies in the fact that, as the voices explain in a manner reminiscent of Nietzsche's philosophy, "all this was once in the future" (I: 39), and especially "because it's not true / that there exist events and things, / phenomena and living creatures not connected / with all the other phenomena and living creatures, / it's not the truth but a lie, / since everything in the world is connected: / whatever you take, is connected" (I: 46). Indeed, everything described here is connected "so mutually, so masterfully, that it takes / one's breath away" (I: 47). Time and space (understood as 'now' and 'here') are meaningless contingencies from the standpoint of the universe; everything unites in the same continuum: "from the vantage point of eternity, / it seems clear that everything [...] / will be mended again, will return to its merry-go-round" (I: 18). Thus, when a voice invokes the motif of *memento mori* by criticizing the anachronistic use of dead languages like Latin and Greek by other voices, they invite him (or her) to abstraction.

Once the subject has been established (i.e., "counting is counting"), "the last thing we need to understand is / how, properly speaking, to think during the discourse, / that is, in what style, in what key" (I: 34). From the *chto* (what) it is time to move on to the *kak* (how). According to the voices, there are three possible lines of reasoning to follow: the first one is that of the wind, advancing in "surges" (I: 35); the second variant is that of the river, flowing peacefully and somewhat mischievously; the third alternative is that of the reed, "scrupulously and accurately" (I: 36). The latter—echoing Pascal's 'thinking reed' as a metaphor for man—is the style chosen by the voices. Pascal wrote that:

Man is but a reed, the most feeble thing in nature; but he is a thinking reed. The entire universe need not arm itself to crush him. A vapour, a drop of water suffices to kill him. But, if the universe were to crush him, man would still be more noble than that which killed him, because he knows that he dies and the advantage which the universe has over him; the universe knows nothing of this. All our dignity consists, then, in thought. By it we must elevate ourselves, and not by space and time which we cannot fill. Let us endeavour, then, to think well; this is the principle of morality (Pascal 1995: 347).

Such is also the reed described in *Triptych*, weak and fragile, at the mercy of nature: "quivery and shivery, shaky and fragile, / and equally lonely" (I: 40). Yet, it alone can understand the hidden rules of the universe, its creatures and phenomena: "the reeds / figured out the most important thing: they understood / that something supposed to happen later, / already happened and ended with creation" (I: 38). As in Pascal, the vanity of wanting to grasp "space and time" is often repeated by the voices in Sokolov's work; the dignity of the thinking reed lies in its ability to think, in its precise thinking that leads to the realization that what should happen has already happened. For Pascal, however, the thinking reed serves as a metaphor for the human being, whereas in Sokolov's text the voices merely strive to think in its style; the voices repeat Pascal's injunction "let us endeavour, then, to think well," but they do not attain individuality. They remain ethereal and undefined vocal instruments in a suspended atmosphere.

Discourse ends with an unexpected and seemingly incomprehensible interruption of the conversation, but this is soon explained. A voice "somewhere, not there at all, and from another lips, / and seemingly about something else, but essentially about this exactly" (I: 45) says: "implacable are the cithers crying in the reeds / of titicaca" (I: 45). Where is the connection with what was said before? The answer given by the voices is clear: if everything is connected, then it is futile to feel discouraged because of the errors, misunderstandings, absurdities of this world since everything has its own reason for being. Those same cithers can cry in the reeds of Titicaca as well as "in the papyri of limpopo" (I: 49).

Discourse ends circularly, with the repetition of the single word *tipa*, "of this kind," that initiated the entire conversation. The voices conversed freely, interrupting each other, resonating, and invoking new themes, such as the circular movement of time, which makes linear movement nothing but an illusion—a theme that has already been addressed in the writer's earlier works.

The voices have further established that everything in the universe is internally related. It is necessary, however, as the true arithmetician knows, to distinguish each object, each phenomenon and each living creature, and to determine for each its proper place, role, and value, and not to generalize, as some "linnaeuses" do, between things that only appear to be similar (such as insects and birds). This is why the call to make a well-crafted list is so important for the voices: if one wants to proceed like a thinking reed, one must demonstrate scrupulosity and accuracy. Not coincidentally, the philornist in the third part of the book works as a "sentinel" in a museum, a place where precise cataloging is essential.

Therefore, *Discourse* is in its own way an anti-Cartesian discourse on method, on the possibilities of thought: in addition to the model symbolized by the reed, there are also the styles of the wind and the river, two recurring elements in the author's earlier novels. Moreover, this is an overtly multi-voiced, polyphonic discourse, conducted by a potentially infinite number of voices who, as they themselves explain, are verbally enacting a musical counterpoint.

From the outset, the title of this first section hints at the book's *raison d'être*: it forms a premise and summary for the discourse that will follow. 'Discourse' here means both form and content, signifier and signified, at once a response to the *chto* and *kak* of the text.

There are fifty stanzas that make up this first section, the shortest of the three: this is the only 'round' number in the work, which may symbolically recall that precision of thought and enumeration to which the dialoguing voices aspire.

Gazebo

The title of *Triptych*'s second section suggests the site of the multi-voiced discourse. In *Gazebo*, however, the conversing voices not only discuss—as in the previous section—the criteria and objects of discourse, but also engage in the process of giving body and "voice" to the creation of Beauty, of 'finesse' (*iziashchnoe*).

Gazebo begins with a brief description, delivered by a voice, of the life and character of Antonio Scandello, a lesser-known sixteenth-century composer (1517-1580). However, the biography of this "*italos*" (II: 2) is rewritten and differs from the original: the historical figure serves, as in any work of art, as a mere pretext for creation.

The most important stages in Scandello's life are mentioned here, beginning with his emigration to Germany (II: 3). As an emigrant artist, "wandering from *vagants* to *sänger*" (*vagantes* and *Minnesänger* being Medieval erring figures; II: 3), Scandello crossed the Rhine and settled on the Elbe, in Dresden, where he became "harmony's *doctor honoris causa*" (II: 3)—metaphorically speaking, he was appointed Kapellmeister here in 1568. For this reason, the voices consult "maestro scandello" to grasp the secrets of artistic creation. Asked about it, the composer replies:

> finesse, you should know, must be virtuosic,
> and it's most correct to create it in arboretums,
> moreover, in pre-dawn ones,
> at any rate, for me,
> and, by the way, to touch upon its aspects too,
> both mentally and verbally (II: 5)
>
> and he said:
> complete darkness there makes you anxious and almost gives you goosebumps,
> particularly in those whimsical kiosks called in some countries gazebos,
> particularly if one touches upon and creates not solos but more or less for voices,
> give it a try,
> only don't forget to show them respect,
>
> otherwise they'll get upset and become silent (II: 6)
> and they wondered:
> but what's so correct about it, pardon us, if there's so much anxiety,
> and he answered them, the envious and fearful:
> the more anxiety—the more virtuosity (II: 7)

Beauty, 'finesse', is said to arise in gardens ('arboretums', *vertogrady* in the original), before dawn and through the interplay of several voices—it is not a *solo* composition. Finesse, then, springs from polyphony—and polyphonic indeed is the counterpoint recalled at the beginning of the previous section.

The garden is also, in its own way, a composite scene: it is a polymorphous place, made up of a heterogeneous set of elements that tune into the harmony of diversity. Grasping the significance of the garden in the text, Vladimir Cherednichenko wrote that the inner space of this literary work is the "resonant multi-voiced garden." Reading *Triptych* can be likened to a slow walk through the winding paths of this garden, returning to our favorite places—only slow readers are able to fully appreciate texts created by slow writers (2012).

In this text, the reader is presented with a concrete garden in which the voices are immersed, but also with a metaphorical one, a sonorous and polyphonic garden that results from the harmony created by the conversation of the voices. The various discursive melodies are its paths, outlined, layered and twisted, recurring with or without variation, and the reader follows them as if in a "slow walk."

Finesse, however, is said to arise not in any garden-space, but "particularly in those whimsical kiosks called in some countries gazebos." Composer Scandello offers a key to understanding the title of this middle section. It is a title that, because of the meta-narrative energy that characterizes the entire *Triptych*, emphasizes the importance of the place for the voices of this second part. If *Discourse* implicitly expressed the content and form of the ongoing conversation (the 'what' and the 'how'), this title identifies the chosen setting (the 'where'); a third section will follow, *Philornist*, dedicated to its self-proclaimed hero (the 'who'). The three titles seem (ironically) to conform to the structural requirements of traditional narratives, indicating plot, genre, setting and characters.

Gazebo, however, is a word that does not exist in Russian (in the original it is written as *Gazibo*): it is the transcription of the English 'gazebo' (another indication of the work's multilingualism)—a choice that underscores the importance of the word's phonetic concretization, spelled literally (in Cyrillic letters) as it is read (in English). In Russian, the corresponding word would be *besedka* (a term that appears as a synonym in stanza 11, along with *kiosk* and the evocative *teatr*), a diminutive of *beseda*, 'conversation', which recalls the title of the previous section, *Discourse*, and describes what the voices do in this particular place.[62]

---

[62] The use of the English term may underline the foreignness of the concept of the gazebo to Russian geography and culture. The first gazebos appeared in imperial parks from the eighteenth century in the course of the Europeanization of the Russian world. This 'westernizing' motif, personified in Peter I (and his Kunstkamera), is developed further in *Philornist*; on closer inspection, however, the entire *Triptych*, in its quotations, allusions,

The gazebo, as a pavilion, is a half-closed, half-open place, in that it is outside (of buildings) and yet inside a garden or park. Its in-betweenness—in-between as the *sumerki*, the twilight—recalls the space of the 'veranda', the literal mythopoeic setting in which the short stories that form the second chapter of *A School for Fools* are written.

The conversation thus takes place under a gazebo—and the garden is indeed a classic setting for art, whether sacred or profane, Western or Eastern. In this literary work, this space regains its status as the main environment for artistic creation, for poetic sensibility.

The voices of *Gazebo*, like troubadours, put into practice the rules originally laid down by maestro Scandello: they meet at night in the gazebo, and "at the very threshold" (II: 10) they introduce themselves by declaring that they wish to converse about some aspects of finesse. Until they notice the "end of darkness," and that "it's getting light quickly" (II: 82), they converse freely, and concretize their artistic creation. As day dawns, the conversation is abruptly interrupted, out of deference to the "treaty of eleven eleven, eleven hundred eleven, / signed between the troubadours and arboretums represented by their voices" (II: 86) which dictates a single but unbreakable rule: "from the break of day to the earliest stars / about finesse—not a sound" (II: 88).

The artistic creation enacted by the voices is extremely musical, as indicated by the number 88, the number of the stanzas of *Gazebo*, which corresponds to the number of the black and white keys of the piano. Indeed, the treaty they mention is the one signed by the troubadours, the bards of sung poetry.

Unlike in the first section, here the composition of the voices gives rise not only to constantly changing images, but also to micro-stories. In discussing "what kind of art" to talk about (II: 23), the voices again emphasize the recurring motif of enumeration: "out of all arts it's best to touch upon the art of accounting" (II: 24). But now this serves as a cue to tell stories: the stories of the arithmetician, the widow, and the officer, which the voices bring to life.

The arithmetician's 'I' is underdeveloped; his direct speeches are almost always introduced by the colon or a verb (such as 'explain', 'hold', or 'inform').

---

images, is a kind of ideational borrowing from European culture and history, from which, Sokolov seems to say, Russian culture is inseparable.

The woman, on the other hand, shifts almost imperceptibly from the third to the first person, making the development of the narrative her own. From stanza 46, when her voice is introduced ("and she says:"), and until her disappearance in stanza 58, the widow becomes virtually the narrator, incorporating into her monologue, where appropriate, the words of the officer, her husband. Finally, the officer narrates his tragic events in the first person, briefly assisted by a fellow soldier.

The arithmetician is a kind of Gogolian "rare akakii" (I: 22) who works "bravely, but quietly" (II: 30) in an office that distributes subsidies to war widows. The widow turns to him, complaining about the small allowance awarded to her, but gets no more than a spark of precarious hope that makes her feel briefly like a bird (II: 41) before she finally turns into a fly, out of desperation (II: 73). A bird and an insect: these are the two classes of animals that a voice had already included in the list of world's creatures as equals in *Discourse* (I: 40) and that continue to occupy a central role in *Philornist*.

As for the woman's husband, he was an unfaithful zoologist who was later called to arms and died in the war. His death is relived several times and in different dimensions, as a captain of semi-cavalry and then as a naval admiral: in fact, he explains that "having fallen, / we are reborn, like some phoenixes, for *vita nuova*, / for new battles" (II: 76). A recurring dreamlike vision—starring his fly-widow dancing in a benefits office—unites the tragic events. If dance characterizes the widow, instrumental music is associated with him, who was drafted in "musical battalions" (II: 53) and died as a horseman-violinist in a kind of battle-concert: "why don't we take a ride at this bleak hour down the enemy's fortifications / and delight him with a concert of heart-rending music" (II: 72).

The transience of life, but also of death, and metamorphosis are motifs that connect all three characters in these micro-stories: the widow transforms into a bird and then into a fly; the officer and his companions are reborn like phoenixes; even the arithmetician, says a voice, was once, in another life, a "sea gypsy" (II: 38), a "filibuster" (II: 79). Time and space, even the epoch seem to change, to transform: "the space that meditated in the style of barocco, / switches to sirocco: / everything becomes washed out, unclear, and seemingly optional" (II: 42).

In short, nothing is final, and yet, a voice notes, in reality nothing disappears forever, as had already been observed in *Discourse*. In *Gazebo*, the voice explains that things disappear only from the "field of external vision" but not from the internal memory, where they often remain painfully indelible (II: 63).

Memory, then, says a voice in *Gazebo*, is the instrument for overcoming death. Indeed, it is this memory that partially survives in reincarnations, even in the case of the characters mentioned above: the officer, though in different lives, always experiences the same vision; the widow's green eyes, her "mesmerizing emeralds" become the "compound" eyes, though green, of the fly (II: 58); the arithmetician, formerly a sea gypsy, shakes the papers in his office as if they were maracas and hums a gypsy song (II: 79).

Memory, which is capable of transcending spaces and epochs, also unites emigrant artists, such as Antonio Scandello, but also Sasha Sokolov. On the one hand, the memory of their work immortalizes them, on the other, they preserve a personal memory of their homeland. In migration, they experience metamorphosis, undergoing a change of skin like snakes, as Sokolov wrote in the essay *In the House of the Hanged* (1983). A few years later, in *A Portrait of an Artist in America* (1986), Sokolov added that the very act of writing is an 'emigration', a moment that torments and marks the artist.

Although the motif of exile in various forms—from the most poetic to the most parodic—is loosely present in Sokolov's earlier novels, autobiographical figures of migrating artists take a central role in *Triptych*. In *Gazebo*, in particular, many 'wanderers' are recalled alongside the Italian composer Scandello: in addition to Medieval *vagantes* and *Minnesänger*, the reader is introduced at the end to some "*pan* matathias" and "*pan* oginski"—as two voices call each other (II: 83, 84). These names might refer to Titus Flavius Josephus (37-100) and Michał Kleofas Ogiński (1765-1833). The former was a prominent Roman historian and writer of Jewish origin, author of works on the history of the Jews, who left Jerusalem—hence "a free man of the levant" (II: 83)—to move to the capital of the Empire. Recognized for his talent and intellect, he was esteemed by the Romans, and Emperor Vespasian eventually granted him Roman citizenship. Michał Kleofas Ogiński was instead an important diplomat and politician of the Rzeczpospolita and the Tsarist Empire. In 1794 he took part in the Kościuszko

Uprising against the Russians, but after it was crushed, he chose the path of exile in France, where he tried in vain to win Napoleon's favor for the cause of the Polish-Lithuanian Confederation. He tried once again to win the favor of Russian Emperor Alexander I, who appointed him senator in 1810: he prepared an 'Ogiński Plan', but the events of 1812 stopped his initiative. Ogiński gradually became disinterested in politics and ultimately decided to spend his last years in Italy (he is buried in Florence). However, he is not only remembered for his political significance: Ogiński was a distinguished composer of Romantic music, author of a polonaise that bears his name. In the stanza recalling the two 'émigré' personalities, Ogiński is described as concerned about the fate of his Poland, while "*pan* matathias" is presented as an individual so 'integrated' that he is not even recognizable by a specific accent. Ogiński and Matathias represent two faces of the fate of those who emigrate, torn between the memory of home and cosmopolitan assimilation. Since these are the two names behind which the voices hide at the end of *Gazebo*, before they take their leave at dawn, they seem to have been conversing from the beginning. These two 'extraterritorial' voices (as George Steiner would put it) recall that particular position from which Sokolov wrote and writes—and, like him, many other generations of artists who recognize their nation, however painfully, only in art. In a song alluded to in *Gazebo* (II: 40), the bard Bulat Okudzhava sang that "Mozart does not choose his own country." Art is stateless and the artist is a perpetual migrant, Sokolov seems to affirm with *Triptych*: art knows no sector, no border, no barrier, nor does it recognize any nationality; it simply speaks and listens to the language of the world, interpreting and reproducing it. Hence the multilingualism, the pluridiscursivity, the pluristylistic character and the constant references to other spheres of art and thought in this encyclopedic and cosmopolitan text.

Philornist

Triptych's third and last part initially seems to differ from its predecessors: there are no intertwined voices, but only one, that of the 'philornist'. This "character"—he describes himself as such (III: 7)—works in a museum not of fine arts, but of fine "beings" (III: 64), a Kunstkamera, though not necessarily the one actually located in St. Petersburg, which is mentioned in the text as an example. He is the "sentinel in the room of insects" (III: 71), although he presents himself as a true philornist, a bird lover, forced to observe these creatures only from the balcony of this museum hall. It is a "sad contradiction" (III: 84), because he sees insects as inferior creatures and is incapable of appreciating them.

What might naively be interpreted as a traditional hero, however, soon reveals its intrinsic ambiguity. Indeed, the philornist—defined by Mikhail Egorov as the "narcissistic narrator" of *Triptych* (2012b)—speaks of himself not only in the first but also in the second person (singular and plural), leaving the reader with the unresolved doubt that there are other interlocutors. He stages a theatrical monologue in which he gives voice to various characters and embodies multiple roles, as he himself explains (III: 11).

It is "after all, theatre," he insists a little further on (III: 18), and, recalling Stein's rose that is a rose that is a rose, he reaffirms that "theatre, / as every gertrude knows, / is, exactly, theatre, / is, naturally, theatre, / is, indisputably and undeniably, theatre" (III: 19). But it is a "theatre of pure reason," "named after immanuel k" (III: 22): here circumstances and the audience are unimportant; time and space are, in defiance of Kant, only provisional and transitory, because, as already been established in *Discourse* and *Gazebo*, the 'here and now' has no meaning from the point of view of eternity. There is only what the philornist calls a "virtual continuum" in which all epochs and all latitudes are intermingled, coexist and overlap (III: 5).

However, the philornist does not seem to be alone in this theater. Indeed, the opening of this section sets the stage for an encounter that proves fundamental to the protagonist's maturation into an aesthete.[63] *Philornist*'s first line reproduces the direct speech of a Hispanic lady, called "the unsightly." *Arrepentios*, she says in Spanish (III: 1). The woman is grief-stricken, unhappy; "reproach flickered" in her eyes (III: 2). She is the only Sunday visitor to the museum who allows herself to disturb the sentinel as he admires the birds from the balcony. She does not,

---

[63] As Sokolov explains, "the philornist is one of those aesthetes who are called artists without canvas, poets without verse. He writes, but not on paper: he writes in the space of his imagination. He considers it his vocation to contemplate birds, to admire them. His sitting on the stool [on the balcony] can be considered a kind of performance; he is a master of ecstatic contemplation of the beauties of this world, is he not an admirer of Zen values?" (Personal communication, email, July 3, 2019).

however, do so with her voice; the woman, the "gaunt *señora*" (III: 25), expresses herself not through words but through the electricity of her chakras, through the fluids of *kundalini* (III: 80). These Sanskrit lexemes recall the idea of the circle, of circularity (in the case of kundalini, the image of the serpent coiled upon itself): this is a recurring motif in Sokolov's work, where everything is interconnected and "was once in the future" (I: 39). However, when the philornist first describes the silent communication of the woman through her inner energy, he also points out that these are terms usually read "in pamphlets about the other-worldly" (III: 4). In doing so, he belittles the sacred significance of these terms and alludes to their use in mass culture, to the commodification and commercialization of yoga practices and oriental philosophies.

The philornist claims to be the only one capable of understanding the lady's esoteric language by virtue of his personal sensibility (III: 26). Later in the text, the reason for the *señora*'s reproach becomes clear: "repent, or you'll be sorry, / since it was probably you / who personally killed all these fine ones" (III: 80). The lady is saddened at the sight of so many lifeless creatures and sees in the sentinel the cause of their deaths. As Sokolov puts it, "the unsightly woman, if you want to see a symbol in her, can be seen as a symbol of compassion, of solidarity with nature."[64]

What seems at first glance to be a 'normal' conversation between two 'normal' characters soon turns out to be silence: the "well-mannered" philornist replies "in good castilian [...] / with a latin bent," yet without saying a word, "silently" (III: 81). Silently, he explains that there are "scientists, experts" who kill these creatures (III: 82)—and he confesses his pain as a bird lover forced to watch them only from the balcony of the room of insects. Silently, the *señora* rebukes him and urges him to look at his situation from a different angle:

don't fall into despair,
you discerned the soundless answer,
because these winged insects,
aren't they in their own way birds (III: 85)

---

[64] Personal communication, email, July 10, 2019.

Winged insects are birds in their own way, that is, they too can be objects of admiration and contemplation; they too are creatures that have reached their own perfection, as was noted in *Discourse*.

Then the *señora* leaves the stage, and the philornist watches her walk off: just as the widow in *Gazebo* was transformed into a fly, so now the unsightly woman—also a widow, it is implied—becomes a bird, a "graceful heron" (*botaurus stellaris*) that lives in the Venetian lagoon and is sung about by the gondoliers (III: 87-89).

The metamorphosis has taken place. What can prevent the reader, if he will, from seeing in this *señora* that fly which he met in *Gazebo*, which now, as if freed from a burden, is awakened to new life, like a phoenix, in the form of an elegant bird?

The motif of transformation, of metamorphosis, finally binds the last stanzas of *Philornist* and *Triptych,* by extension. The philornist suddenly disappears, and with him the backdrop of the museum dissolves, while the discourse focuses on this heron "of the adriatic waters" (III: 87), on whose scales the iridescent lights of the night are reflected, like mother-of-pearl and tourmaline (III: 91-94). They are the lights of the waterfront lamp, the carnival fireworks, the torch, and finally the ephemeral (and Pasternakian) match—again the importance of lists is emphasized. These lights are temporary, precarious, unstable, just like their reflections on the lagoon and on the bird. They are lights and shadows intermingling, dying and being reborn, preparing a suitable setting for the appearance of the character who brings the reading to its conclusion.

In these last stanzas the figure of a gondolier-*cicerone* who looks like Celentano appears (III: 96): his match, used to light a cigarette, reflects off of the heron. This gondolier comes from the Venetian island-cemetery San Michele (III: 95); he, Sokolov explains, "gets up from his grave at night to move around, to warm up, to meet the tourists, he is bored there on the island."[65] For him, death does not represent the end, a constant idea in Sokolov's work.

Triptych ends with a farewell between this character and some voices, his clients, whom he has led to the threshold of a Venetian trattoria:

---

[65] Ibidem.

and, having lit up,
our celentano said to us quietly:
ciao,
and we answered respectfully:
arrivederci (III: 99).

Such a conclusion does not have the finality of an ending: we can imagine the gondolier waking up on other nights and encountering new voices—and a 'goodbye' (*arrivederci*) is not a 'farewell forever' (*addio*), after all.

Philornist's 99 stanzas leave the discourse in a suspended state, and this number is par excellence a symbol of imperfection, of the opening to the infinite, of the unclosed circle.

Triptych begins with a conversation devoted to the method of thought, dialogue, and creation, and ends with the artistic composition—not on paper, but in the "virtual continuum" (III: 5)—of an aesthete serving in a museum, which is the spatial concretization of the recurring Leitmotiv of enumeration in the work. In this room, insects—perfect creatures (I: 40), fine beings (III: 64) like all others, to return to the model of the thinking reed (I: 36)—are listed, ordered, cataloged, and displayed for present and future visitors. After all, they are as worthy as birds: they have simply reached different stages of evolution, of metamorphosis; even the fly may become a graceful heron in another life. As the voices that gathered in the night at the gazebo announced, every creature is destined to be reborn again and again, like the mythical phoenix (II: 76), burdened by the painful baggage of memory (II: 63). And what better place than the "multi-voiced garden" (II: 82), the Edenic, polymorphous, sempiternal, lush nature, to remember this? The present time is a transient, passing theatrical stage; the 'great time' is instead an immeasurable eternity in which everything comes to life again. It is the eternity of the night, of the garden, of the stars—a floating time that communicates itself musically through those voices that read it and become its resonating instrument.

Sasha Sokolov's baroqueness

The previous section has attempted to summarize the interpretive tools that aid in the study of the four books of Sasha Sokolov. Taken together, these investigations support the notion of 'classification difficulty' discussed above. There is evidence of the presence of features that can be described as modernist, postmodern or, more generally, avant-garde, experimental. However, applying any of these terms to Sokolov's entire oeuvre leads to simplification. This section will conclude the study by providing a summary of the main characteristics that constitute Sokolov's poetics. Avoiding the above-mentioned labels, I choose to define this set of features as belonging to a specific 'Sokolovian baroqueness', welcoming the suggestion made by Pyotr Vail' and Alexander Genis back in 1980.

Vail' and Genis's interpretation of Sokolov's work was wholly original and *sui generis*: five years before *Palisandriia* was published, the two critics wrote an article on what they defined as "parasite-literature"—an entirely new literary practice, situated "between prose and poetry, esoteric, aristocratic" (1980: 214). In this article they proposed the definition of "Soviet baroque" (*sovetskoe barokko*)—among its representatives they included Sokolov, Aksyonov, Maramzin, Dovlatov, Yerofeyev, Popov, Aleshkovsky, and Vakhtin. Vail' and Genis observed some similarities between the prose of these authors and the baroque art of the 17th century—the latter is characterized as such:

> The joy of life is absent, as is the certainty of man's victory; the tones of pessimism, of skepticism, of the uncertainty of life resound ever louder. [...] The depiction of painful suffering, morbid or base passions, horror and filth is brought to the fore. [...] Instead of regular simplicity and integrity, [...] an extreme complexity, mosaicism, metaphors and whimsical similes (1980: 222).

According to the two critics, the abundance of common elements justifies the use of the label Soviet baroque:

> The Soviet baroque conceived in the 1960s hastened to describe life. Everything found its place in the baroque—the only thing missing was the civic spirit, a strong hero who understood the personal goal as a social ideal. And other models appeared: Bulgakov, the OBERIU, Platonov's distorted syntax, Zoshchenko's tales. And then, the stream of consciousness, the Europeans, the Americans... The baroque hero searches for the truth too, but it is unknown which one, it is unknown where, and whether it exists at all. This hero lives as if he were outside society and his own epoch. [...] The writers of the second half of the 1970s—whether Yerofeyev, Aksyonov, Sokolov, or the authors of Metropol'—are idealists. They are intensely searching for God, but their way of doing so is profoundly unconventional for Russian literature. [...] In their search for their own divine soul, they move away from reality, passing through metaphysics and mysticism, through eroticism as self-knowledge, as self-mastery, through openness and the "everything is allowed." On a formal level, the baring of the device has become the norm. The mimetic formula ("as in life") has disappeared altogether, replaced by a new principle: "Literature has as much value in itself as life, and this is how it is constructed."

The author has entered the narrative rudely and unceremoniously, the hero is split into a series of doubles, real names and addresses have made their way into fiction... (1980: 222-223).

In this article, the critics figuratively sketched the narrative structures of the works of the representatives of Soviet baroque. To represent Sokolov, they drew concentric circles that do not touch, do not contaminate, but are contained within each other, reproducing the effect of a pebble thrown into a pond: "Circles form on the surface, but no one threw the stone. There was no stone" (1980: 228). Each inscribed circle carries some deformed original elements and acquires new properties, which it in turn passes on to the next inscribed circle, and the next circle brings all the received material back into play and metamorphoses it. This Chinese box structure (or matryoshka doll system) is more than a literary device, it is the authentic architecture of Sokolov's novels; truth always remains unattainable and deferred due to the chain of infinite circles.

The Baroque classification has also been used by other scholars of Sokolov's prose, notably the aforementioned Mario Caramitti (2002: 26; 2019: 415) and Olga Matich, but Johnson too wrote of *Palisandriia* that "the writing reflects many stylistic registers, but a parodic imperial baroque is one of the major voices" (1986a: 640). Matich, in a recent article presented at the annual ASEEES conference, emphasized that elements such as symmetry, reflection, and specularity are indeed closely related to Baroque aesthetics (2017). Again, however, some baroque traces in Sokolov's work are not sufficient to label this author in general terms.

To conclude this investigation, it is important to determine what features may define Sokolov's poetics. This set of features, then, will describe what might be called a specific 'Sokolovian baroqueness'—not a calculated adherence to the baroque sensibility of the 17th century, but rather a personal reworking and elaboration.

Sokolov's texts are structured like networks, with multilayered plans connected by intricate, spiraling threads. The reader is given clues and 'riddles' to reconstruct the lines of interpretation. Artistic creation, even when it assumes minimal forms, is not averse to accumulation—but one that is piled up vertically (in depth), not horizontally (in length). Metamorphosis, mirrors, and masks as motifs and narrative devices serve such a vertically 'condensed' structure, and the same is true of intertextuality. Boundaries are erased while lines of connection are emphasized and always in progress, opening up to different languages, alphabets, subjects, disciplines, and arts (including ekphrasis). Morphology and syntax function in the same way since form and content are an indissoluble unity and allow the coexistence of multiple facets.

Other elements—such as the presence of an unreliable narrator, the playful relationship with the reader, the defamiliarizing artifice (concretized in particular by the recurring twilight), the emphasized connection between signifier and signified—may locate Sokolov's work within specific traditions and sensibilities. However they ultimately characterize this specific 'Sokolovian baroqueness'.

In terms of genre, Vail' and Genis had already observed a tendency towards an in-between of prose and poetry in Soviet baroque: in Sokolov's case, this in-betweenness takes the forms of *proeziia*, a theme explored further in Chapter 4.

Chapter 3.
Pictures from an Exhibition

> "Music seems to me to act like yawning or laughter."
> Lev Tolstoy, *The Kreutzer Sonata*

In a letter dated January 22, 1984, Sokolov's publishers, rattled by a recent mail squabble concerning royalties, sharply reminded the debut author[66] that "Ardis did not get rich from your books, and does not expect to" (Mss 117, Box 1: 7). Indeed, Sokolov's books never became a sensation outside of literary circles. Although his first novel, *A School for Fools,* was widely translated[67] and still represents a reference point for much of contemporary Russian literature (and theater),[68] the audience this author has reached throughout his literary career predominantly consists of elite readers. Sasha Sokolov himself voiced discontent in this regard, acknowledging that "there are only a few readers for my literature," thus reclaiming his own "right to strike" (Vaiman 2003), that is to say, to maintain a prolonged silence following the publication of his last novel *Palisandriia* in 1985.

---

[66] Following Sokolov, renowned debut authors at Ardis have included Sergei Dovlatov (*Nevidimaia kniga, The Invisible Book,* 1977), Aleksei Tsvetkov (*Sbornik p'es dlia zhizni solo, Collection of Pieces for Life Solo,* 1978), Vladimir Uflyand (*Teksty, Texts,* 1978), Vladimir Paperny (*Kul'tura Dva, Culture Two,* 1985).

[67] *A School for Fools* has been translated into English (1977, 2015), German (1977), Dutch (1978), Polish (1984), Swedish (1984), Serbian (1988), French (1991), Portuguese (1993), Danish (1994), Spanish (1994), Estonian (2005), Italian (2007).

[68] Cynthia Simmons maintains that Sokolov's voice may be heard in much literature of the 1990s, e.g. in Narbikova's as well as Sorokin's texts (1993: 3). Novelist Mikhail Shishkin admits having "long walked in Sasha Sokolov's shadow" (Orobii 2012), and the same has been acknowledged by writer Dmitry Danilov (2017). When *A School for Fools* first appeared officially in the Soviet Union, Riga-born writer Andrei Levkin authored *A Short Story entitled Sasha Sokolov* (1989), a homage to the author. More recently, Mariam Petrosyan's novel *The Grey House* (2009, trans. 2017) may represent a latest example of Sokolov's influence on contemporary Russian literature. As far as theater is concerned, *A School for Fools* has been adapted for the stage several times, including in 2011 for Lena Sheveleva's innovative dance theater production (see also Marchesini 2012b); in 2006, director Andrei Moguchy, introduced Sokolov's second novel, *Between Dog and Wolf,* to the stage after having successfully produced his dramatic version of *A School for Fools* (1998).

When Sokolov's more minimalistic texts appeared on the pages of the Russian-language Israeli journal "Zerkalo" in the 2000s, either critics and readers failed to notice him. Yet, in the introduction to his meticulous English translation of the collection of essays and vers libres *In the House of the Hanged*, Alexander Boguslawski writes that Sasha Sokolov is "arguably the most original Russian writer of the past four decades," "acknowledged in the West and in Russia as a ground-breaking innovator, a literary maverick, an unsurpassed master of the Russian language, and an ingenious stylist, whose enormous importance for Russian and world literature is unquestionable," making him "perhaps the most important and influential living Russian author" (2012: vii-viii). Why has such a prominent writer failed to reach worldwide success and recognition outside of elitist circles of Slavists and devoted aesthetes?

Language—as the foundation of composition and as the artistic result of a "linguistic dance" (Gureev 2011: 165)—both enriches Sokolov's texts and limits their accessibility to readers. Although Sokolov is widely recognized by critics as a master in crafting and nurturing his own language, a systematic investigation of how language works in his oeuvre, and of how the author's understanding of linguistic creation shapes his texts is still missing. The objective of this chapter is to examine and explain the authorial theory of literary creation in relation to Sokolov's works. The analysis requires reflection on the role language plays in the syncretic idea of artistic creation put forward by Sasha Sokolov. On the most elementary level, language is the primary tool of a writer, but it is also instrumental as a means of engendering artistic creation, which transcends the arbitrary distinction among art forms including music, visual and performing arts. Although all of Sokolov's texts are taken into consideration, this chapter primarily focuses on the process of verbal composition in his last published book *Triptych* (2011).

A language to compose texts

Numerous studies have argued that there is an unambiguous relationship between the central axis of Sokolov's literature and the author's take on language and its power. Importantly, Sokolov himself has never concealed this point; instead, essays like *The Key Word of Belles-Lettres* (1985) and *The Anxious Pupa* (1986) clarify his position. Sergei Divakov (2013) carried out investigations into Sokolov's early production (short stories and articles published in the Soviet press and student almanacs between 1967 and 1971) and demonstrated that such idiosyncratic use of language—including particular attention to the form and continuous play with sound correspondences—can be traced back to these writings. However, it is undoubtedly in the following three novels and especially in his last work *Triptych* that Sokolov's literary technique reaches full maturation.[69] This maturation suggests conscious and ongoing reflection by the writer on language as "both a tool and a philosophy" (Podshivalov 2006: 357), accompanied by his sound knowledge of rhythm and meter of the traditional Russian verse.

Generating words

Pyotr Vail' and Alexander Genis (1993: 14) suggested that Sokolov's writing exemplifies "language pantheism"; his "pregnant" words continuously give birth to other words, objects, images, figures, and characters. The sudden emergence—in the middle of a "slovarnyi potok," a verbal torrent (Johnson 1982: 168)—of Veta Akatova,[70] the biology teacher and love interest of "student so-and-so" in *A School for Fools*, is one of the excerpts most frequently quoted and examined by critics. Names acquire a particular value in Sokolov's oeuvre, recovering traditional links with the sacred act of naming (Chantsev 2012). Ontologically, they reveal semantic connections with the outer world.

Such reverence for naming, as well as Sokolov's own emphasis on the influence of the Bible and Christian tradition on his work, directly encourage parallels between Sokolov's literary cosmos and the Christian tradition of baptism. However, critics have often failed to catch the importance of holy texts

---

[69] Sokolov's poetic prose—cadenced, rhythmic, and rich in alliterations, rhetorical figures, internal rhymes, paronyms—has fascinated scholars; see for example Yuri Orlitsky's analysis (1997), Siergiej Kormiłow's investigation (2011) and Noemi Albanese's dissertation (2017).

[70] The character is generated by the following word-sound associations: "vetka zheleznoi dorogi" (a branch of the railroad)—"vetka akatsii" (a branch of acacia)—"Veta/Vetka Akatova". Later in the same passage the name of Veta is intertwined with the image of the willow ("vetla"), of which she becomes a branch, but also with the Russian alphabet, according to which *veta* corresponds to the third grapheme.

and religious motifs in his oeuvre. The Bible naturally represents a reference point, a formal lyrical model for the author. While not a practicing Christian, Sokolov admits that being "born and raised in a Christian country," he "reason[s] according to Christian categories" (Kochetkova 2017). In a recent interview he maintains that "among the list [of world masterpieces] the best books are indeed missing," implying the meaning and beauty represented by the New Testament and the Gospels. The formal value of the Holy Scripture is something that "even believers often fail to grasp" (Vrubel'-Golubkina 2011).[71]

The divine attribution given by Sokolov to the creating word ("in the beginning was the Word") emerges in particular in his treatment of proper names (his own included[72]) in his novels (Johnson 1984; Toker 1987; Johnson 1989: 164; Iablokov 1997: 207; Caramitti 2001: 119-120; Boguslawski 2006). Sokolov's word-processing conceptually recalls the Adamic and Shakespearian preoccupation with "what's in a name."

As first observed by D.B. Johnson, the epigraphs chosen for *A School for Fools* have the purpose of "alerting the reader to certain central devices" (1980: 229): while two of the three epigraphs focus on the nature of proper names—"Saul, also known as Paul" (Acts, 13:9) and "The same name! the same contour of person!" (E.A. Poe, *William Wilson*)—, the remaining epigraph draws the reader's attention to the phonetics of words with regard to its mnemonic utility, by pairing a set of irregular Russian verbs (known by heart by any Soviet pupil) with a song chorus or refrain: "гнать, держать, бежать, обидеть, / слышать, видеть и вертеть, / и дышать, и ненавидеть, / и зависеть, и терпеть"[73] (to chase, to hold, and to rotate, / to hear, to see, and to offend, / to run, to breathe, likewise to hate, / and to endure, and to depend). These epigraphs suggest the

---

[71] The biblical echo in Sokolov's *proeziia* will be further analyzed in the next chapter.

[72] Not only did he abandon his first name Alexander (Aleksandr) for the diminutive—or "pseudo-name" as Oleg Dark has defined it (1992: 225)—Sasha, thus putting on a different mask in emigration, but his name is recalled in all the titles of his novels (Dark 1992). The presence of a recurring ornithological motif can be linked to a continuous play around his last name Sokolov since *sokol* is the Russian word for the falcon (Marchesini 2012a: 63).

[73] The verbs form a quatrain composed of trochaic tetrameters—a scheme typical of oral and folkloric poetry that is characterized by a strong musicality and frequent alliterations (Jakobson 1966: 420; Gasparov 1996). Sokolov reworks this form in his *Between Dog and Wolf* (Smith 1987).

prominence that names and words acquire—graphically, phonetically, semantically—in the book. The paratextual position of this list of verbs highlights Sokolov's deeply intentional approach to language and helps to establish the important role that words play throughout the narrative. Indeed, the first sentence of *A School for Fools* emphasizes this idea: "Right, but how to begin, with what words?" (2015: 7).

In Sokolov's novels the characters and the (always unreliable) narrators become what Mario Caramitti calls "poly-characters" due to their unstable and fluid identities (2002: 26). The authority of proper names is questioned, as characters are split, doubled, mirrored,[74] disintegrated and reassembled. We read, for example, in *Between Dog and Wolf*: "And in Ploski among more or less runners one can find the youngster Nikolay who never had his own name or, more precisely, had, but too long ago" (2017: 8); "But ain't clickin, somebody suddenly said, ain't smartin over there, in Ploski, that Fyodor, on the abacus of his? That is, not necessarily Fyodor but sorta Pyotr. And, in general—Yegor" (2017: 10); "Listen, where in the world did I find such a last name, where did I snag it? Maybe I'm a Gypsy baron or maybe the wind simply blew it in" (2017: 200). The treatment of names aligns with the subjectivity that characterizes Sokolov's literary cosmos (Freedman 1987; Matich 1987; Vail', Genis 1993). However, this destabilizing process does not imply that the act of naming is devoid of meaning. Instead, Sokolov's narrators facilitate reflection upon the primal value of proper names, suggesting that *"there's much* in a name."

The power(s) of language

"But only say the word and I shall be healed" is the formulaic utterance heard before Communion is administered during mass. Words have the power to heal and to save in Sokolov's cosmos. As Johnson has observed, positive characters in *A School for Fools* "are related to the wind (and to each other) by common phonetic elements in their names and in their associated motifs" (1980: 225); thus, in this case, as 'wind' corresponds to 'veter' in Russian, it is the syllable *ve-* which guides the healing process (*V*eta Akatova, Roza *V*etrova, Medv*e*dev, Pav*e*l

---

[74] Olga Matich has recently developed an analysis of the mirror's presence and role in Sokolov's oeuvre, concentrating on *Palisandriia* in particular (2017).

Norvegov). These "children of the wind" are saved in accordance with the windy association[75] they carry along in their proper names. By contrast, most negative characters are given foreign names (headmaster Perillo, doctor Zauze), which are impossible to decline according to Russian grammar. However, critics have failed to recognize that the bizarre names bestowed on these intrinsically negative characters empower them to condemn and deplore.

As for the headmaster, his name may recall the historical figure of Perillos (Perilaus in Greek, Perilai in Russian) of Athens, a bronzist in classical Greece (6th century BC), who was killed by his own creation—a torture machine. It is possible that Sokolov wished a similar fate for the school's principal, creator of the much-despised "slipper system," a real torture for pupils. Given the central role of entomology in Sokolov's writing, it is also interesting to note that the term *perillus* indicates a particular species of predatory bugs.[76]

Doctor Zauze's name references Sokolov's biography: Zauz'e is in fact a small village located in the Ostashkov district (Tver oblast), only 125 miles north of Bezborodovo, where the writer lived and worked as a gamekeeper in 1972-1973, when writing the novel. It is in this area, in the Valdai Hills, that the Volga—the river *par excellence* in Russian literature and a prominent element in Sokolov's second novel *Between Dog and Wolf*—originates. When Doctor Zauze threatens to send the "student so-and-so" to that mythopoetic and vague "over there," Sokolov may have in mind the remote and arcane village symbolized by his name.

Finally, it seems significant that the school vice-principal's last name, Trachtenberg, recalls that of the Russian mathematician and engineer Yakow Trachtenberg (1888-1953), best known for the rapid calculation system[77]

---

[75] Arnold McMillin later observed that "incidentally, [the geography teacher] Norvegov is also referred to semi-anagrammatically as Vetrogon in connection with the theme of the cleansing, purging wind [...]. Freedom [...] is associated with whiteness, transparency and, particularly, the wind" (1990: 233-234).

[76] Professor Akatov's research in *A School for Fools* deals with entomology, while the "student so-and-so" collects winter butterflies. Sokolov's essay *The Anxious Pupa* also could be considered in this regard. The interest in entomology evidently unites Sokolov and Nabokov.

[77] *Sistema bystrogo schyota po Trakhtenbergu* (The Trachtenberg Rapid Computation System) was translated and published by Prosveshchenie publishing house in the USSR in 1967. This publisher provided all Soviet educational institutions with school textbooks.

that bears his name. Alternatively (or at the same time), Trachtenberg is also the last name of an early 20th-century adventurer named Vasily (?—1940). In 1908, he published a brilliant collection of *blatnoi zhargon* (*Blatnaia muzyka*), which includes linguistic material collected in various prisons of the Russian empire, in spite of the fact that he was neither a linguist nor a lexicographer. The choice of the name Trachtenberg can no longer seem coincidental when we consider that the second name given to this double character is Tinbergen, the last name of Nikolaas Tinbergen (1907-1988), founder of modern ethology, who, together with Konrad Lorenz and Karl von Frisch, received the Nobel Prize for medicine in 1973 "for their discoveries concerning organization and elicitation of individual and social behavior patterns." The Trachtenberg-Tinbergen character therefore bears intertextual names that frame her activities as vice-principal. On the surface level, her role focuses on education, control, rules and surveillance, but the possible reference to Vasily Trachtenberg and his work also points to the importance of approximation and abjection.

Apart from the aforementioned connections to historical figures, graphically and phonetically these names generate further associations. If the vice-principal Trachtenberg reminds the reader of that sound refrain "tra-ta-ta" that is associated with her crippled walk—a refrain that, as Mario Caramitti puts it, sounds like a "funeral sex march" (2004b: 114)—we should not exclude that the last name Perillo possibly contains a reference to the idea of danger, of peril, of something indeed *perilous*.[78] Indeed, the form of Sokolov's words is inextricably linked to their intrinsic content. Moreover, Trachtenberg's "tra-ta-ta" march circularly evokes the image of the train, which apart from being a constant symbol in much Modernist literature, represents a key element in Sokolov's "Twilight Cosmos" (Johnson 1986a: 647). Just as Veta Akatova is explicitly born from the seeds sown by the sounds of language, phonetic imagery shapes Sokolov's narration: "But you see, phonetics is the yeast, the fermenting agent of language. I start with a sound; sound is like a grain from which everything else grows," the writer maintains (Podshivalov 2006: 357). The reader must learn to listen properly and carefully to these so-called phonetic grains.

---

[78] English words happen to be present in the novel, exemplified by the lyrical 'nightingale'.

If we turn to the second epigraph[79] chosen by the author for his successive novel, we shall notice another hint that, although previously ignored by critics, compels us to reassess the value of auditory abilities. "The young man was a hunter": this short quote from Pasternak's *Doctor Zhivago* seems to refer trivially to the book's structure, which envisions a cycle of poems authored by an anonymous "Binging Hunter." However, this specific quotation occupies a particular spot in its original literary source: the "young man" it talks about is the interesting interlocutor with whom Zhivago converses while on the train. Once in the dark of the night, the interlocutor turns out to be deaf and, therefore, capable of sustaining a conversation solely by lip reading. This pivotal sequence in Pasternak's novel unravels the theme of incommunicability, a topic that is of great interest to Sokolov too. By evoking the idea of the power of language and of its sound, which not everyone is capable of hearing, Sokolov once again stresses the redeeming sacredness of the word. After all, this seemingly epistolary second novel by Sokolov presents itself as a letter addressed to detective Pozhilykh by Ilya Zynzyrela (later discovered to be dead), in which the sender seeks justice for a wrongdoing. Thus, the writing offers a refuge and a redemption from (linear) time and death.[80]

In the following novel by Sokolov the protagonist and autobiographer Palisandr again suggests that redemption can be achieved through the written word, though not without skepticism:

> Yes, we writers have an easy time of it! A scribble here, a scribble there, and zap! you're immortal. Well, not *you*, perhaps. [...] The impression, widespread among certain overwrought individuals, that one need to do have one name's enshrined for the ages is die—that impression has no basis in practice (1989: 17-18).

It is not by chance that in a chronicle like *Palisandriia*, one of the recurring motifs—imbued with a Pasternakian ringing[81]—is "smerti net," there is no death.

---

[79] The first epigraph is an excerpt from Pushkin's *Eugene Onegin*, to which the novel owes its title.

[80] On the idea of circular time and death in Sokolov's oeuvre, see Boguslawski (1987).

[81] "There shall be no death" (*smerti ne budet*) was in fact one of the variants evaluated by Pasternak for the title of the novel that we know today as *Doctor Zhivago;* on this topic, see Vadim Borisov's work on the genesis of this text (1990). Italian scholar Irina Marchesini proposes an examination of the nullification of death in Sokolov's novels in the

Like a resounding echo, the word remains alive in Sokolov's cosmos, fleeing temporality.

A sound architecture[82]

When Tatyana Tolstaya in 1988 first officially introduced Sokolov to the Soviet public on the pages of *Ogoniok*, she emphasized the "sound architecture" of his writing:

> The word that he throws generates an echo that resonates for a long time through the pages; it does not extinguish itself, it mounts, gathering other words around itself, and, all summoned in the resonant building of the book, they sound like a close-knit, fused, radiant, and passionate chorus (1988: 21).

Similarly, the German scholar Georg Witte has attempted to outline the circular movement of construction and deconstruction through which words are generated in Sokolov's echoing torrent: what at first is a definite word, in a second phase is stripped of its meaning, thus dissolving into a scream, into non-existent signifiers, into undifferentiated noise, but only in order to be subject to a final reshuffle that gives birth to a new word, sometimes a true neologism (1989: 118).

Sokolov's words are then able to conceive and generate new sounds and new meanings, thanks to their signifier, their sound-image, their phonetic and graphic value. Such linguistic birthing is presented by the writer as something highly spiritual and sacred as it relates directly to an idea of pure Beauty and Truth, epitomized for example by the emergence of the beloved Veta Akatova, but also by the "student so-and-so"'s merging into a water lily (Nymphaea alba).

This typically Sokolovian "maieutic" (obstetric) treatment of language as a potentially infinite game[83] of linguistic birth and rebirth has been connected by some critics to the sacred-mystical writing and translation technique of the

---

light of the OBERIU tradition, in particular considering Kharms and Vaginov's reflection on death, art and immortality (2018b).

[82] Parts of this subchapter and the next one have appeared in an article published in Russian in "Voprosy literatury" (Napolitano 2021).

[83] Sokolov affirms that "literature is but a game," and that, in comparison to his native Russian, which he molds like modeling clay, "English is not a flexible language, there are no cases, inversion in the order of words is problematic. Moreover, there is a mass of useless words, articles for instance. This is why English is not suitable for the game to which I am accustomed" (Erofeev 1989: 198).

Tarnovo literary school: the so-called *pletenie sloves*, word weaving (Kopeikin 1985; Marchesini 2012a, 2018a). If for the medieval monks the sacred word relates to the divine, then for Sokolov the word creates Beauty and Truth, giving access to a fully sacred level of being (Vail', Genis 1986b: 161).

Such word weaving emerges as an evident stylistic trait in Sokolov's last work *Triptych*, where the structure of the discourse—conceived "as a continuous flow of words"—is, according to Marchesini, "reminiscent of the 13th- and 14th-century Bulgarian experience" (2012a: 67). The Italian scholar maintains that a certain "expanded polysemy" of terms allows in this text for a strong link with the literary tradition, while proposing a restoration of the antiquated and elegant genre of belles-lettres. However, while it is true that such "expanded polysemy" permits language to continuously generate visual associations, analogies and metaphors, such examination fails to draw proper attention to the specific role played by signifiers in Sokolov's writing. It is in fact not only polysemy (and therefore the meaning of linguistic signs) which creates images, but more often signifiers that give birth to new visual pictures. Sokolov's words are creative in a primordial sense, by virtue of their sound alone. Thus, his writing closely resembles the work of a composer.

When asked to elaborate on this topic, Sokolov clearly explained:

> I use language as if it were music, in particular my language. Sound, assonances, euphony are all extremely important to me. The problem, though, is that very few people are able to read my texts correctly. Most do not hear the music.[84]

For the *proet*, language is first of all music. As the writer has affirmed many times, the plot is not of much importance to him;[85] what guides his linguistic and literary composition is the uninterrupted pursuit of the proper sound, the perfect intonation, the music of Russian language, the mother tongue he has enriched with neologisms and loanwords according to the specific needs of linguistic harmony.

---

[84] Personal communication, email, December 17, 2017.
[85] "The subject: this side of literature has never attracted me. The subject is an artificial thing, the subject is a commodity for sale. The way language works is important to me, this sort of linguistic dance. If I had been born in another time, in another place, in another family, I would have become a composer, because language is one of the forms of music" (Gureev 2011: 165).

I compose words. When I see that words do not match well, I do not use that pair or trio of terms. They must reference each other not only by their intrinsic sense, but also by their sound. This evidently resembles the work of a composer. Perhaps, I could have been a composer if I had been born in a musical country, although Russia certainly is. But if I had grown up, let's say, in Austria, I would have become a composer of classical music; I would have written symphonic music. Language is music given to us from above, but we often do not appreciate this fact (Kochetkova 2017).

In such word weaving, the traditional notions of rhythm and meter naturally acquire a key role, as they represent the intrinsic 'musical' tools of language. The importance of tradition in Sokolov's literary activity (both evident in the iterated intertextual references found in his works, and in his direct comments disseminated in interviews and the essays) also informs his writing technique. Even when graphically resembling plain prose, Sokolov's texts are not devoid of metricized passages. In the 'vertical' structure of *Triptych*, the first section in particular—*Discourse*—hosts a wide range of traditional syllabo-tonic meters.

Listening to the linguistic symphony

Sokolov subverts the idea that music resembles language in its form and structure.[86] Rather, it is language, conceived in a primal manner as a code deprived of content (of narrative subject, of plot), that is inherently a form of music, as demonstrated by traditional poetry with its rhythm and accents. Language is able to restore its original ties with music only once its superimposed layers of meaning are ripped off. For the *proet*, this music-language represents "the only place where being new is still possible" (Podshivalov 2006: 357).

Elsewhere the writer has stated that every literary work "must sound like a symphony" (Vrubel'-Golubkina 2011), but in order to appreciate this verbal symphony one must understand its sonic alphabet, which requires a rare ability. As for Sokolov, he claims to have perfect pitch:

Since childhood I have had a good ear, I have perfect pitch. I sang well. They even invited me to join the choir at the Bolshoi theater, but I refused due to the idea of being ashamed in front of my friends, my schoolmates, who could have said: here comes the little singing

---

[86] Treatise writers of the 17th and 18th centuries even believed in the possibility of compiling 'musical-rhetorical treatises' on the model of treaties devoted to poetry and oratory (Pagnini 1974: 18).

bird, let's say. I hear language very well. I write according to the sounds (Kochetkova 2017).

Apart from singing, Sokolov recalls taking accordion lessons in his "childhood, boyhood and youth,"[87] an instrument that the writer put into the hands of his first literary narrator "student so-and-so." The boy's father in *A School for Fools* is very critical of the son's music teacher,[88] yet he is not the only one unable to appreciate the art of music. In Sokolov's *proeziia* sound occupies a prominent place: *proeziia* is (like) music, Sokolov says—"without an intonation you cannot get anywhere."[89]

It must be for this reason that Sasha Sokolov has a special admiration for avant-garde poet Velimir Khlebnikov, whose work he considers much more complex than his own: "It takes several years of preparation to understand Khlebnikov, but it is well worth it. After Khlebnikov, Sokolov will be easy" (Podshivalov 2006: 358).

For Sokolov, Khlebnikov, who in words saw both *zvuk* and *razum*, sound and sense (or, literally, reason),[90] represents not only a model for his style and approach to language. He embodies the figure of the Poet, the artist *par excellence*. In 1985, Sokolov dedicated a short text to Khlebnikov, that he read on the radio, in honor of the centenary of the poet's birth; this literary work is the result of the encounter between the two poets' discourses.

> Khlebnikov. In this destiny the issue concerning 'the artist and society' expressed itself in all its irresolubility. Art is a means enabling the understanding of the inscrutable ways. The artist predestined to wander along them is an *Agasfer* [the wandering Jew]. He is a living and wandering hieroglyphic question mark. The questions he poses to the world have no answer. And therefore, his hunchback cannot be fixed. The arrival of *Agasfer* gives people anxiety. And, if not openly, then in a hidden way he is persecuted. For Tsvetaeva: 'Every poet is a Jew.' For Sinyavsky: 'The writer is always and everywhere an enemy.' And, it is clear, the most superfluous people of all times are not the Pechorins

---

[87] Personal communication, email, December 17, 2017. The playful reference to Tolstoy's trilogy is obvious in this statement.

[88] "If it were up to me, I would make them, those fake Mozarts, scratch to a different tune [...]; if it were up to me, I'd make him play the trumpet where he's supposed to" (Sokolov 2015: 151).

[89] Personal communication, email, January 10, 2019.

[90] Sokolov himself maintains that "it's impossible to speak about phonetics separately from meaning. Linguistics captures that notion in the term *zvukosmysl* [sound/sense]" (Podshivalov 2006: 357-358).

and Onegins, but the Lermontovs and the Pushkins. Being a poet for poets, Khlebnikov was and remains a superfluous among the superfluous, an outcast among outcasts. But time carries him with it (Pomerantsev 2013).

A Jew, an enemy, a superfluous figure, even an "heretic" as Evgeny Zamyatin defined him: this is and must be the Poet, according to Sokolov. He lives within the language, rather than in society,[91] which regards him with suspicion and disappointment. The figure of the Poet recalls the one of the legendary wandering Jew (or Buttadeus), traditionally condemned to carry the entire *Weltschmerz* (world weariness) on his shoulders.[92] The figure of a valiant Buttadeus (*udaloi butadeus*), appears in *Triptych*:

> wandering thinker, rebel, chimney sweep,
> he trumpeted about it from roofs and troubadoured from cornices,
> he knocked inspired at any door
> and, finally, the biographer notes, knocked himself out:
> so be on your radiant, milky way, enchanting roamer,
> cut down by authorities for lunacy and ravings on art (II: 18)

Just like all poets-Jews, *Triptych*'s Buttadeus suffers a miserable destiny. The philornist (literally, a bird lover) that is the protagonist of the third section of Sokolov's last work is an aesthete capable of understanding the poetry of birds by watching them from the balcony. The philornist deeply admires the harmony of their *zaum* (the futurists' language of birds, or "ptichy iazyk"), as an unhappy museum overseer—a "sentinel" (III: 66)—in the room of dead insects. Perhaps it is precisely the fact that the insects do not emit a clear and distinct sound of their own—as they are lifeless bodies, on display in the hall of a museum—that makes them so abject (initially, at least) in the eyes of the philornist. Nature does not

---

[91] Olga Matich defined Sokolov as an "inner émigré who ended up in emigration" (1987: 302): fleeing from reality, seeking freedom to express himself, Sokolov found in literature a favorable environment to cultivate his artistic word; in this environment he feels no more as a 'foreigner'. The artist is in fact, according to Sokolov, essentially *chuzhoi*, a foreigner, a stranger to the surrounding world; "living outside of time, of space, of any place, he lives only in himself" (Polovets, Rakhlin 1981: 8). The word has thus become home to Sokolov's erring soul. In language only he lives by right, mixing life and literature: experience crosses fiction, while author and character tend to—albeit fictionally—overlap.

[92] The figure and the legend achieved great popularity in Europe over the centuries, especially in the arts. In Russian culture he is better known as *Agasfer* (Vsevolod Ivanov, for example, authored a *povest'* entitled *Agasfer*). Viktor Toporov defined Sasha Sokolov as a "Russian *Agasfer*" (2009).

seem to want to communicate anything through them. Instead, nature communicates through the wind and the river, common motifs in Sokolov's literary cosmos (together with birds)[93] that, as noted by Irina Marchesini, "produce a specific sound" (2012a: 61). Sokolov's baroque garden of correspondences should then be read out aloud (or listened to),[94] paying due attention to its rhythm, sounds, and music.

Triptych's music

A major advantage of selecting *Triptych* for the purpose of investigation is that this text allows a deeper and comprehensive insight into Sokolov's linguistic construction by virtue of three main reasons. First, being the last published work and having followed a prolonged silence of the author, it may be considered as the most mature *result* of the writer's literary activity. Second, as stated by Sokolov,[95] *Triptych* represents the ultimate point in his personal artistic research and may thus be taken as a *manifesto* advancing Sokolov's views on the process of literary creation. Lastly, it is the book in which *music* most evidently takes the lead, as music influences content and form.

The musical element appears in a twofold nature in the book. On the one hand, key works and figures related to the history of world (European) music are repeatedly mentioned; on the other hand, the text itself suggests a cadenced, rhythmic reading, a musical interpretation. The sustained presence of straightforward references to music—mentions of composers, instruments, compositions—, accompanied also by the use of a specific terminology (often in Italian) invites the reader to carefully re-read the text in order to gradually notice the musical allusions that are initially less obvious.

For ease of analysis, it is possible to divide the historical figures of world music and the musical pieces recalled in the book into four different strands: in the first, the Italian composer Antonio Scandello stands out as the 'metronome'

---

[93] The ornithological presence in Sokolov's oeuvre has been investigated by M. Ziolkowski (1987), I. Marchesini (2012a), J. Vergara (2021).

[94] Russian audiobooks of *A School for Fools*, *Palisandriia* and *Triptych* do exist, the latter being read by the author.

[95] "*Triptych* is the result of years of work. Some of its pages are, in my opinion, the best I have ever written. Especially *Gazibo*" (Kochetkova 2017).

of the text; the second strand includes all the musicians and, especially, the compositions which perform a poetic function in the book, being terms of comparison within metaphors, intertextual hypotexts, or object of ekphrasis; the third strand comprises the tradition of sung poetry, such as troubadour poetry; in the fourth strand we find the poets for whom music plays a fundamental role and who are therefore, in a certain sense, Sokolov's predecessors (among them, first and foremost, Federico García Lorca). After examining the way music enters the *proetic* composition in *Triptych*, we shall turn to the investigation of how a specific kind of verbal music is created in the text.

Antonio Scandello: a metronome under the Gazebo

The musical figure who assumes the most significant role in the structure of the book is the little-known sixteenth-century composer Antonio Scandello. In fact, it is "maestro" Scandello, at the beginning of *Gazebo* (*Triptych*'s second section), who indicates the modalities according to which Beauty (*iziashchnoe*, finesse) shall be created:

> finesse, you should know, must be virtuosic,
> and it's most correct to create it in arboretums,
> moreover, in pre-dawn ones,
> at any rate, for me,
> and, by the way, to touch upon its aspects too,
> both mentally and verbally (II: 5)
>
> [...] the more anxiety—the more virtuosity (II: 6)

His words become a rule to be followed and implemented in the course of the voices' dialogue.

Undoubtedly his name, today almost forgotten, represents a poetic pretext in *Triptych*. We shall hypothesize that Sokolov chose Scandello for this reason:[96] if

---

[96] Sokolov affirms having found information about Antonio Scandello in an encyclopedic volume devoted to music: "I think I read about him in a music encyclopedia. I was amazed by his biography. Just imagine being born and raised in mythical and inspired Italy, and then in the full blossom of your life you emigrate to Germany and live there for good: that's how far money and comfort desire can take you." Personal communication, email, July 10, 2019.

he had opted for a well-known name of European music, he would have bound the character to their historical identity and biography.

Scandello's words open the second section of the work; they function as an epigraph around which the conversing voices who gathered in the night garden reflect, poetically weaving their polyphonic composition. However, the details of the composer's life and work are intertwined with this poetic function in Sokolov's book.

Antonio Scandello, born in Bergamo, Italy (then Republic of Venice) in 1517, was a composer, musician and cornett player. In 1549 he was invited by Duke Maurice Elector of Saxony in Dresden to join the city orchestra then directed by Johann Walter; the Kurfürstlich-Sächsische und Königlich-Polnische Kapelle is one of the oldest orchestras in the world that is still active today. Scandello was not the first Italian to become a member of the Kapelle. His brother Angelo, a timpanist, joined him in 1553. After a brief stay in Italy to flee the plague, Antonio Scandello was appointed Kapellmeister (chief conductor) in Dresden in 1568, enjoying great fame and success as a teacher, composer and instrumentalist until his death in 1580.

In Sokolov's text, the composer's biography is sketched vaguely and unfaithfully. Scandello is generically referred to as an "*italos*" and "a child of rubicon" (II: 2, 3). The reference to this river (which does not flow near Bergamo) is justified by the following metaphor: "in his youth, / [...] he crossed the rhine" (II: 3), reenacting the famous Julius Caesar's river crossing, in order to finally settle on the Elbe, the river flowing through Dresden.

Before mentioning his status as a composer, the maestro is defined as a "quite delightful street falsetto" (II: 3). The Russian term here employed, *diskant*, actually plays around a false friend of the musical jargon: in Russian, it indicates the treble voice rather than the proper *discantus*. *Discantus* is one of the very first forms of medieval counterpoint, which splits the melody between a low voice and a higher voice that proceed homorhythmically. If the Russian term suggests the young age of maestro Scandello and the timbre of his voice as a child, the Latin term recalls the "counterpoint" (I: 3) of polyphonic composition, touched upon in *Triptych*'s first section, *Discourse*.

Indeed, Scandello himself authored religious polyphonic music (a musical language at the height of popularity at the time in Europe). His *Johannespassion* (1561) is based on the Passion according to the Gospel of John. The choral sections of Scandello's *Passio*, in German,[97] are articulated around a structure divided into the four parts typical of 16th-century music, which are sometimes reduced to three or multiplied by splitting. It is interesting to note that the Evangelist's voice is radically different from the others: his solo part, in fact, follows a non-mensural notation system (though on staff), almost a psalmody, that shall be interpreted according to Gregorian monody, where the rhythm is marked by words. This choice amplifies the hybrid nature of Scandello's composition.

Besides this work, Scandello authored the first volume of Italian songs published in the German-speaking world, *Il primo libro delle canzoni Napolitane*. The first volume of the collection (1566) contains songs for four voices (*discantus* included), while the second volume (1577) comprises songs for five voices too. In *Gazebo*, once maestro Scandello has indicated the criteria for the creation of Beauty, the conversation continues by mentioning this composition of his:

why not exit, like in one of his *canzoni*,
wondrous *canzoni alla napolitana*,
singing it silently on the way,
la-la-la-la, let's say,
why not step out, *donnerwetter, in den geliebten garten* (II: 8)

Scandello, the protagonist of *Gazebo*'s first eight stanzas, is thus present both as a historical figure and as a poetic pretext for the introduction of new motifs. His appointment as maestro—an inspirational model for the voices conversing in this section—is justified by his biography and work. Polyphony, his own emigration (at the age of thirty-two like Sokolov), the presence of Christian motifs in his oeuvre, and the songbook—written in Italian but published in Germany, like Sokolov's Russian books published through Ardis in Michigan—are all elements that make him a suitable addition to *Triptych*'s (and Sokolov's) world. The difference between Scandello and the other names mentioned in the text lies

---

[97] At the time, Dresden had already embraced Protestantism: *Passions*, which in Italy appeared less frequently in this period, experienced great popularity in Protestant Germany. The choice can be explained with the intention of detaching the German church from the Catholic one also in terms of sacred music, sung in German, rather than Latin.

in his active role in the plot: the maestro turns into the proper 'metronome', according to which the voices gathered in the night garden sing their poetry.

Music enters poetry

As they converse, *Triptych*'s voices often directly mention the name of famous musicians, composers, singers—from Chopin to Monteverdi, from Ogiński to Celentano. Moreover, they also make more or less explicit references to classical and popular compositions, both Russian and international. The references to some classical romances, such as *Kalitka* (Gate) and *Para gnedykh* (A Pair of Bays) may appear obvious, especially to the Russian reader. A voice, for example, invites "at the very threshold of the gazebo [to] give your name" (II: 10), just as it is sung in the first romance: "where the branches are more thickly woven together, / there I'll wait for you, at the gazebo, / and at the very threshold of the gazebo, / I'll take off the lace from your sweet lips." In the third section, *Philornist*, on the other hand, we read that "you were a conscientious master of a pair of bay" (III: 58): as in the musical piece, the voice continues the wordplay, keeping the noun 'horses' implicit.

Oblique, but nevertheless detectable, are the references to the German patriotic song *Die Wacht am Rhein* ("he crossed the rhine / and with the watch, / first with the third, then with the fourth, / the watch of these currents and bends"; II: 3) and to the very anthem of Germany ("*über*, as they say, *alles*"[98]; III: 10).

References that would not be immediately understandable are clarified, such as those to the song—perhaps *La biondina in gondoleta*, set to music by J.S. Mayr, L. Beethoven, R. Hahn—sung by the Venetian gondoliers: "whom the gondoliers of the adriatic waters / so deftly celebrated in one of their erotic *arioso* // *la-la-la-la*, they sang, / *la-la-la-la*, / ragazza piccola mia" (III: 87-88).

These musical references serve various functions in the text. If the direct allusions, for example, to *Kalitka* and *Die Wacht am Rhein* seem to be purely citational (here the musical pieces are conceived as literary hypotexts), the German anthem and the Venetian song function instead as terms of comparison.

---

[98] "Deutschland über alles" is the first verse of the anthem, which is no longer sung today. The current anthem includes only the third stanza of the text written by A.H. Hoffmann in 1841.

In particular, both appear within a metaphorical construct relating to birds. The philornist, commenting on his own handwriting, states that it is reminiscent of insects—a woodlouse when writing in Latin characters, a scolopendra when using Cyrillic ones. Both, however, try to imitate the speed of a bird, he says, and not just any bird, but the one that, in fact, is *über alles*—the falcon:

> and not simply,
> not even simply the feathered,
> but the kind
> that possesses nearly the most praiseworthy features,
> *über*, as they say, *alles*,
> flying, in the squint of the meticulous philornist,
> *i.e.*, bird lover,
> if not with the swiftness of the wild pigeon,
> then at least of the kestrel, of the saker,
> with circafalconian, colleague,
> with circafalconian[99] (III: 10)

The *ragazza* described by the gondoliers in their "erotic *arioso*" is a heron, that *botaurus stellaris*, into which the *señora* turned at the sight of the philornist:

> she'd leave the museum,
> by her stature and gait
> and her haughty smile resembling the one
> whom the gondoliers of the adriatic waters
> so deftly celebrated in one of their erotic *arioso* [...] (III: 87)

> we are talking, of course,
> about the Venetian marsh bittern
> *botaurus stellaris*,
> relatively small, woeful,
> but at the same time quite a graceful heron,
> whose grey plumage morphs into purple (III: 89)

Thanks to the musical reference, the falcon and the heron acquire particular connotations. In the first case, in the eyes of the philornist, the bird emerges above the others in a proud, almost arrogant manner, that is, like Nazi Germany, which made that first verse of the Lied, written when the German state did not yet exist, a manifesto of national and racial superiority. In the second case, the woman,

---

[99] In Russian, the last line reads "s okolosokolinoi": an obvious allusion to Sokolov's last name. The fact that the author inserts his own name into these stanzas, in which he mocks the philornist's writing, is subtly self-ironic.

initially "unsightly" (III: 1), becomes a heron whose grace and sensuality inspires an "erotic *arioso*."

Finally, certain quotations are translated from music into language in *Triptych*. The officer's story is a case of ekphrasis, in which the battle is transformed into a concert:

> i woke up, wanted to calm down with arpeggios:
> it didn't work,
> my guarneri is clearly in a bad mood, can't be tuned:
> probably, says my adjutant, from humidity,
> after all, he says, fog's all over the place (II: 71)
>
> [...] friends, angels,
> why don't we take a ride at this bleak hour down the enemy's fortifications
> and delight him with a concert of heart-rending music,
> and:
> march-march through overgrown water-meadows,
> march-march (II: 72)
>
> and as long as, blasting the radetzky, we pounded the hooves in the dale,
> everything was going *très bien*,
> but as soon as we started galloping up and down the knolls playing in memory of elise,
> [...] the fog dissipated,
> and the night turned to be as moonlit,
> as chopin's *nachtstück* in c-minor,
> opus, if i am not mistaken, twenty something,
> and it's finished,
> we were discovered and:
> with shrapnel, with shrapnel
> and so mercilessly, unceremoniously,
> do you remember, old pal bassoon, our disappointing demise (II: 73)

The officer-violinist acts as an orchestra conductor and proposes to his comrades that they break through the enemy ranks at night with an unexpected attack. The invitation to march through the valley merges with the cadenced *Radetzky March*; but everything goes wrong when Beethoven's lighter, more relaxed piece sweeps away the fog, and the night is illuminated by the moon; here *Für Elise* fades into *Op. 27 No. 1*, one of Chopin's best-known nocturnes, with its delicate, vaguely melancholic character. The officer and his companions are thus fatally discovered by their enemies.

The tradition

The tradition that binds poetry and music is ancient; the separation between the two arts is artificial. In *Triptych,* the voices do not see barriers and distinctions in artistic creation and turn to models and masters belonging to worlds conventionally conceived as distant. In particular, *Gazebo* references the *clerici vagantes*, *Minnesänger* and *troubadours,* who constitute the classical figures of the medieval tradition of poet-musicians.

Sokolov's Scandello is said to have left Italy in his youth, "wandering from *vagants* to *sänger*" (II: 3). He is, in a sense, both a prophet (for the voices) and a devoted disciple to the rules for the creation of Beauty, which turn out to be derived from an ancient *courtly* agreement allegedly signed in 1111 between troubadours and gardens (II: 86). Even his slightly parodic and anachronistic search for a soul mate recalls the medieval tradition of courtly love:

> and having no luck in a particular sphere,
> he often thought in a minor key
> and his ad announced: (II: 3)

> a certain *italos,*
> smiley, middle-aged, bachelor,
> will establish a lofty relationship with a *frau* of good repute,
> preferably zoftig,
> though he's concerned he has little experience in such
> because for years he has endlessly made music (II: 4)

The insertion of these references to the tradition of sung poetry acts as a clue for the reader, as the work stems from this tradition. As such, in order to appreciate the text, the reader must first understand how to read it: in *Triptych* "everything is musical" (Kochetkova 2017).

Poets and music

Many writers and poets—from Proust to Kafka, from Mann to Joyce, from Pushkin to Blok[100]—have approached music in a natural, instinctive way in their

---

[100] As far as Russian culture is concerned, the Italian Slavist Ugo Persi noted that "Russian literature, which almost always accompanies philosophy, when not support it [...], never introduces a musical theme with an autonomous or purely hedonistic function. We can say that the musical theme is intrinsic to the ethical-philosophical one, and that for this reason

verbal creations, not recognizing boundaries between the arts. Sokolov, especially with this last work, merits inclusion in the list. However, there is one specific poet who has always represented a model for Sokolov due to a natural proximity of their sensibilities: Federico García Lorca.

The influence that the Spanish poet has had on the Russian writer is deep and lasting: quotations from Lorca can be found in *A School for Fools* and Sokolov's short graphic composition *Duende* (2006) is a homage to the Spanish poet (Napolitano 2020b).

References to Lorca are also present in *Triptych*. In the first section, for example, there is an explicit allusion to a "sleepless and merciless" guitar "crying to honour" a certain "federico garcía" (I: 13). The strings of this guitar are linked to the long and painful torment caused, according to one of the conversing voices, by delays: the metaphor initially arises from the assonance between the Russian terms 'provolochki' (delays) and 'provoloki' (strings). A new intertextual reference is added to this image, which recalls Lorca's poem *La guitarra*:

Empieza el llanto
de la guitarra.
Es inútil
callarla.
Es imposible
callarla.
Llora monótona
como llora el agua,
como llora el viento
sobre la nevada.

The crying of the instrument is inconsolable in this poem, as we read in *Triptych*. Moreover, in Lorca's text, the guitar cries monotonously like water and wind. Those two natural elements—omnipresent in Sokolov's cosmos—are regarded within *Triptych* as embodiments of possible 'styles of thought', in addition to that embodied by the reed (I: 34-37).

The guitar is a recurring image for Lorca that the writer frequently personifies and complicates with additional meanings, as in this poem. The instrument

even in an apparently insignificant poem there are motifs that go well beyond the representation of a worldly entertainment, carrying instead values of greater cultural, social and historical interest" (1999: 58).

immediately recalls the poetics of the *cante jondo*, the primitive, primordial, spiritual *siguiriya* gypsy song, which begins with a terrible cry and continues with the "lágrima sonora sobre el río de la voz" (Lorca 1922). This is the song of the Duende according to the Spanish poet; it is close to the "trino del pájaro, al canto del gallo y a las músicas naturales del bosque y la fuente," and it is not found in the throat, but "sube por dentro desde la planta de los pies" (Lorca 1922). This is the origin of authentic poetry and music; it is the Aleph of sound that guides both Lorca and Sokolov's artistic research, recreating the "primer llanto" and the "primer beso" (Lorca 1922). For Sokolov, this is the result of his profound devotion to language, from which he cannot escape, as he poetically expressed in 1986 in the essay *The Anxious Pupa,* which Johnson has called "a meditation on the prison-house of language" (2006: 240).

The reference to ancient and modern traditions alike establishes a line of continuity between Sokolov's work and the work by other poet-musicians who understood the importance of harmony.

Composing verbal music

Music is not only present in *Triptych* in the form of direct and indirect quotations related to composers and compositions. The entire text is in fact assembled as if it were sheet music in terms of its vocabulary, rhythm, and resonance. The iterated presence of musical jargon—a presence that is frequently made evident by the Italian origin of this vocabulary, and by the graphic use of italics, as in the case of *piano*, *amabile*, or *vivace* (I: 1, 6, 26)—underlines *Triptych*'s attachment to this art. The *recitative*-like reading advocated for by the voice who opens the literary text (and by the writer too, who expects the reader to interpret it through a "glissando"[101]), then reveals the rhythmic structure of the verses. The words, in their syllabic composition, turn into notes, whose length determines the rhythm of the textual symphony. Especially in *Triptych*'s first section, this rhythm frequently arises from the perfect adherence of Sokolov's verse to certain meters of Russian syllabo-tonic poetry: this tradition does not represent a strict rule for

---

[101] "The intonation of my [verse] is colloquial, light, it can and should be read in a glissando." Personal communication, email, July 10, 2019.

the voices in composing their polyphonic dialogue, but it is rather a frame of reference.

This structure applies beginning with the very first stanza in *Triptych*, which is enclosed by verses composed by a series of short alliterative syllables, reiterating sounds and marking a tight rhythm: "tipa togo, chto, mol, kak-to tam, chto li, tak"[102] (of the kind that, say, somehow, perhaps, this way) and "to-to i to-to, to-to i to-to, to-to i to-to, / i prochee, ili kak otsekali eshchyo v papirusakh, / etc" (this and that, this and that, this and that, / and so forth, or like the abrupt cuts in ancient papyri: / etc) (I: 1).

The end of the first stanza presents the series of "to-to" that works almost as a refrain in *Triptych*: the particle *-to*, often repeated in the pronouns 'kto-to' or 'chto-to' (but also 'te-to', that is to say someone, something, those), accompanies the reading of the text. Such a cadenced opening sequence imposes a certain reading: it is not accidental that, shortly after, the dialoguing voices comment on the list of "to-to" here presented by using precise musical terms, "counterpoint" included (I: 3).

The musicality and rhythm established by the repetition of the plosive (occlusive) consonant in short syllables—something that can be easily found in Sokolov's previous works too, particularly the pronoun and adjective 'ta' (that one)—resonate similarly later on in the text in that "tá-ta-ta tí-ta-ta" that is a direct quotation from a poem by Maximilian Voloshin,[103] *V vagone* (In a railcar). In stanzas 29-32 of *Discourse*, a voice metaphorically describes the list of "to-to" by drawing a parallel to the 'music' of the train on tracks—not just any train, but the one sung by this "southern versifier" (I: 30), whose "noteworthy / century" has been carried away "by the wind of history" like a sheet of paper, beyond the windows of the railcar: "and so, it flickered beyond the windows very *vivace*, / lively: tá-ta-ta tí-ta-ta, tí-ta-ta tá-ta-ta" (I: 32). The accent put on the first syllable

---

[102] Accented syllables are the fourth, seventh and twelfth, with a caesura after the fourth.
[103] Maximilian Voloshin (1877-1932) was not only a poet, but also a well-known landscape painter. Many of his works depict the enchanting Crimean spaces around Koktebel, a holiday resort much loved by Sasha Sokolov (Maxim Gureev's 2007 short documentary movie starring the writer *A peizazh bezuprechen...* was filmed here). In *Triptych*, it is stated that this "tí-ta-ta tá-ta-ta" is "painted" by the poet ("zhivopisuet poet") and "the landscape is flawless" (I: 33).

establishes the only possible reading: this rhythm, concretized by reading out loud, verbalizes the railway music that originates in the "to-to" list that opens *Triptych*.

Apart from the recurring alliteration of the plosive consonant, figures of sound involve the whole structure of the text, concatenating stanzas situated even at a great distance from one another. Sounds often determine the development of the discourse, or condition the occasional use of foreign words: the "fly-*frau*" (in Russian "mukha-*mujer*") that is the female protagonist of the officer's premonitory visions in *Gazebo* (II: 79), derives her suitable appellative from the assonance between the Russian and Spanish terms (in Boguslawski's translation between the English and the German ones); elsewhere, the Spanish verb *esperar*, employed as a synonym for *hope* (*upovat'* in Russian), introduces the term "esperanto" (II: 39).

Words and images are linked in the text as they would be in a musical piece, in which the melody alone is capable of evoking visual and emotional associations in the mind of the listener. The sound and rhythm of syllables recall other syllables, to which new meanings are connected: this is a typical technique of word weaving in Sokolov's oeuvre. Words turn into inspirational sources that generate new images.

If we look at (or, rather, listen to) *Triptych* as sheet music or a polyphonic concert performance, in which different melodies follow a specific development, then the words that make up the melodic phrases of its musical discourse can be properly read as notes on the staff. Just as in a composition, they follow one another rhythmically regardless of their meaning, repeating some sounds and varying others, opening to digressions, returning to certain points, insisting on certain timbres.

The aforementioned railway music itself works in this sense: the cadenced list of "to-to", says a voice in the text, recalls the train schedule (*raspisan'e*), or more precisely the assonant (in Russian) description (*opisan'e*) of a railway journey. The entire passage in Russian is built around sound repetitions and variations:

> vernee ne raspisan'e, a opisan'e
> poezdki po takovoi, kakovoe chitaem
> u iuzhnogo stikhotvortsa togo zamechatel'nogo
> stolet'ia, chto tol'ko chto, vot te na,

> uvlechyonnoe vetrom istorii, otletelo,
> chto nazyvaetsia, proch, otletelo bezdumno,
> budto by nekii list (I: 30)[104]

Words or expressions may act as contextual refrains, thus connecting different and distant 'melodies': the reader, in finding something familiar, is guided by the reading process. In the third section *Philornist*, for example, the *arrepentios* (repent) repeated by the *señora* to the protagonist and accompanied by a set of other recurring expressions works as a refrain and connecting tool, linking the main melody of their conversation to various discursive digressions: "*arrepentios*, / she used to say, appearing in rooms and halls, / in halls and rooms of a certain museum"; "repent, / advised the unsightly one in something drab, / appearing in the halls and rooms, / repent, / she spoke with her *kundalini* to you and others in the museum" (III: 5, 23).

Besides serving as a connecting device, the repetition of similar, alliterative syntactic structures has the function, in turn, of marking the rhythm of the reading, creating natural caesuras and emphasizing identical and different accents: "pora postupka, pora postupleniia nastupila, / stupai zhe"; "kogda vy eshchyo ne nuzhdalis' ni v pensii, ni v pensne, / i spesivitsy vashikh lestnits i ulits nosili takie tanketki, takie fufaiki, tuzhurki, / v karmanakh zhe—pis'ma s nevoli, da alkogoli, / da kurevo, da nozhi" (I: 20; II: 15).[105]

Finally, a frequent refrain among *Triptych*'s voices first appears in stanza 27 of the first section *Discourse* and is then repeated several times by different voices in the same terms or with some variation: "counting is counting, / inventory taking is inventory taking" ("perechisliat' tak perechisliat', / uchityvat' tak uchityvat'"). This 'counting motif', like the refrain of a song, implicitly reiterates the rationale that binds all digressions, images, and speeches, namely, the need to draw up an accurate list, in which insects and birds are not mistakenly mixed, where every

---

[104] "more likely, not about the schedule, but the sketch / of a trip on such a railroad, we read about / in the works of a southern versifier of this noteworthy / century who quite recently, would you believe, / carried by the wind of history, flew, / as the saying goes, away, without a thought, / like some kind of leaf."

[105] "the time for your mission, the time for admission has come, / go, don't miss it"; "when you needed neither a pension nor a pince-nez, / and the haughties of your staircases and streets wore such platforms, such hoodies, such jackets / and in their pockets—letters from captivity, and *aqua vitae*, / and smokes, and knives."

item and idea (including errors, "misprints," "slips of tongue, changes of mind, / blunders of memory and imagination"; I: 48) is placed in the correct spot, according to the scientific rules that order the catalogs of museum collections.

In *Triptych*, synonymy and paronymy make these lists concrete:

> but i'd like to remind you of something at once,
> of what, of the fact that the list of this kind
> is sometimes called an inventory or a register,
> it's called exactly that: a register or an inventory,
> an inventory or a register, and some also say:
> a balance sheet, a balancing sheet (I: 11)

> and do you remember, my friend,
> how in the light of the waterfront lamp,
> carnival fireworks,
> a torch,
> or, perhaps, a beacon
> the scales on her feet opalesce (III: 90)

> [...] it's completely logical,
> and yet a blunder crept into the given recollections:
> considering the sources of light,
> you did not include in the listing
> the match of our *cicerone*,
> a swarthy smoker from the island of san michele (III: 95)

The multiple series of homophonic terms and the sets of words with adjacent meanings are the result of such a prescriptive refrain.

In summary, the repetition of sounds, words, expressions, and syntactic structures steers *Triptych*'s contrapuntal, polyphonic composition. Repetition both introduces a dominant rhythm to the reading and connects the text to different and distant 'melodies'. The cantillation-like intonation, a form of "glissando" as Sokolov himself proposes, develops through the rotation and interchange of conversing voices[106] who reiterate and vary themes and timbres, polyphonically interweaving motifs that generate pictures and scenes. The results achieved in *Triptych* represent the most mature example of the search for natural and elegant

---

[106] The philornist's role in the composition may be considered similar to that of an aria singer in an opera.

verbal (linguistic, phonic) harmony that has defined Sokolov's research since his first texts.

Voices on stage

Although some previous studies have dealt with Sokolov's idiosyncratic use of language, researchers have not defined the 'background' and 'results' of such treatment in much detail. Having discussed in the previous section how the use of language in Sokolov's oeuvre reveals a particular authorial understanding of artistic creation (the 'background'), the following part of the chapter investigates the 'results' of such a "linguistic dance" (Gureev 2011: 165).

A gallery of still images

As Sokolov openly stated in the essay *The Key Word of Belles-Lettres*, the form (the how, *kak*) is more interesting to him than the content (the what, *chto*), a priority that has defined the quality of his works. Erasing the traditional idea of *siuzhet* (plot), viewed as the organization of motives and sequences, Sokolov's narration develops through a spiral chain of associations composed of sounds and images.

The graphic aspect of words and (Cyrillic) letters by itself facilitates additional word weaving, as happens for example in Sokolov's second novel:

> With the letter *ge*, shares Pyotr, we came up without a problem; it resembles the gallows, it does, 'cuz on the gallows you can pronounce only that letter: *ge*, *ge*, and *ge*. The letter *de* is like a dacha, *be* almost like *ve*, and *ve* almost like *be*, but *zhe*—that one's mysterious. [...] Well, said Krylobyl, sniffin his sleeve as a chaser, what kind of sound can be heard at the Wolf River, when one of our grinders starts workin on his grindin stand, ain't it *zhe-zhe-zhe*? Exactly. That's why I am askin, Krylobyl continued talkin to Pyotr: The wheel from the grindin stand, which is lyin in the dust of this sickler turned upside down, ain't it sorta-kinda the sought letter? (2017: 44, 46).

The effect achieved in the reading process is that of a suspended atmosphere of still, frozen pictures in pastel tones, slowly interchanging, following a montage pattern, and communicating sensations and perceptions, rather than defined ideas. The reader is thus taken through an art gallery, as the title of some sections in Sokolov's second novel *Between Dog and Wolf* suggests: "Pictures from an

Exhibition".¹⁰⁷ It is not a coincidence that this title also identifies the homonym cycle of ekphrastic piano pieces by Russian composer Modest Mussorgsky (1874),¹⁰⁸ stressing once again the conceptual link between different art forms—word, image, and music.

As one committed to the reestablishment of direct links between the arts, Sokolov admits being more than satisfied with the choice his Moscow publisher OGI has made concerning the insertion of illustrations when re-printing his three novels: "Galia Popova's illustrations are wonderful. She has understood everything and got it all."¹⁰⁹

With the publication of the unusual fragment composition entitled *Duende* (2006), a unicum in his oeuvre, Sokolov reached the highest point in his practice of 'writing through images' that he has cultivated since the beginning of his career (Napolitano 2020b).

The seemingly simple title of Sokolov's last work, *Triptych*, is key to understanding the vast and ancient artistic tradition to which Sokolov refers, as it suggests a sacred, ritualistic¹¹⁰ union of literature, music and figurative art. Russian medievalist Dmitry Likhachev affirms that "word and image were more closely linked in ancient Rus than they are in the modern age" (2009: 51). In *Triptych*, Sokolov reestablishes the antique syncretic harmony of Beauty, typical of a pre-Cartesian—and not only Russian—conception of the world, as a book meant to be read and interpreted, whose single elements assume meaning only in connection with the others. This guiding thread runs through *Triptych* and binds

---

[107] To provide an example from the same novel: "To draw the distant silhouettes of the post office employees—letter carriers, gripped by anguish and the leaf fall. [...] To draw from memory the bottom of the ravine, overgrown with ferns, and the dam holding the reservoir of drinking waters [...]. To draw a passenger station [...]. To draw the heavy, nebulous, slovenly face of Maria and frequently, instead of the expected portrait, may the inexperienced draftsman create the image of her mask, as it were; and the mask wanted to wake up, to come to life, but its tormenting lethargic debility turned down to be stronger than its feeble wishes—it did not wake up" (2017: 17-19).

[108] The title is most often translated in English however as *Pictures at an Exhibition*.

[109] Personal communication, email, December 17, 2017. Some of these illustrations have been reprinted in Napolitano 2018.

[110] The Orthodox rite, moreover, highly regards the value of sound harmony, repetition, and order.

together the three parts that compose it. The choice of such a title goes in the same direction.

The book is made up of a continuous and evident intertwining of quotations that are both intertextual and intratextual. Often, this substratum of texts offers a useful guide to following and interpreting the flow of the voices' discourse.

Among the different hypotexts, there are also sources belonging to non-verbal art forms. Intertextual contexts include, on the one hand, the world of music (possibly the most evident and omnipresent), and on the other, the theatrical scene linked to images and symbols in the book.

Moreover, the scenic "backdrops" change continuously in *Triptych*: the reader is taken from Lake Titicaca to the Venetian lagoon, from a view of the Japanese willows to a visit to the Coliseum in Ancient Rome. In this way, *Triptych* brings the sound element to the foreground, while simultaneously playing with the visual material. The title, which refers both to the sphere of music (and musical theater), and to that of figurative art, hints at the fusion of sensory modes needed to participate fully in the book.

In the history of music, the best-known triptych is possibly the one composed by Giacomo Puccini, consisting of three one-act operas: *Il tabarro*, *Suor Angelica* and *Gianni Schicchi* (1918).[111] Puccini's tripartite creation was inspired by Dante's *Divine Comedy* and was suggested by writer Giovacchino Forzano. Beyond the structure, the protagonist of the last act is also derived from Dante's masterpiece (condemned in canto XXX for "personal falsification"). Puccini's three operas belong to very different genres—tragic, lyric, comic—, thus presenting the spectator with a diversified compendium of emotions and operatic situations. Contrast is the dominant feature of this particular *Triptych*.

Turning now to the visual field, and in particular to figurative art, a triptych is generally understood as a specific form of polyptych consisting of three folding

---

[111] Sergei Rachmaninoff also authored three one-act operas: although not conceived as a triptych, the three operas—*Francesca da Rimini* (again a Dantean subject), and the Pushkin-based *Aleko* and *The Miserly Knight*—share the same short form, typical of the time. Through one-act operas, composers endeavored to overcome the clichés of 19th-century melodrama. As for Puccini, he reluctantly accepted that the three acts of his *Triptych* were performed separately, but because of their intrinsic diversity this was the most popular representation from the beginning.

panels facilitating transport, typical of sacred art and Orthodox iconography. Usually, the center contains a depiction of the Madonna and Child, while the saints are neatly arranged on the sides. In the Orthodox tradition, the triptych closely resembles the royal (or holy) doors (*Tsarskie vrata*). During mass, officiants move through the main opening of the iconostasis, which, by extension, is a symbolic representation of the gateway to heaven.

However, other famous triptychs do not have sacred origins: the Dutch painter Hieronymus Bosch (1453-1516) authored visionary (and almost pre-surrealist) polyptychs that have fascinated experts in diverse fields of art and science, including psychoanalysis. Bosch was also a source of inspiration for Pieter Bruegel the Elder, the painter of *The Hunters in the Snow,* which plays an important role in Sokolov's *Between Dog and Wolf* (Johnson 1982, Caramitti 2000, Baknina 2015, Napolitano 2018). *The Garden of Earthly Delights* triptych (ca. 1500) is Bosch's masterpiece. Art critics are still divided regarding its interpretation. Some consider the painting—particularly its central panel—to be a moral admonition against human sins, while others instead interpret the painting as a Dionysian celebration of the lost paradise. Hans Belting, commenting on the human figure that may represent a possible self-portrait of Bosch, has emphasized his ironic gaze, an expression that can serve as a "signature of an artist who claimed a bizarre pictorial world for his own personal imagination" (2005: 38). Bosch's triptych is full of vivid and detailed figures covering the entire altarpiece (*horror vacui* was typical of the pre-modern and baroque mentality). The interpretation of such a dense artwork, partially due to a general lack of information concerning the biography of the author, is difficult, if not impossible.

Triptych's polyphonic discourse is set in a similar 'garden of delights'; in this garden the voices have the opportunity to freely implement their conception of Beauty. If *Duende* is thus the graphic result of Sokolov's reflection upon artistic harmony, *Triptych* is its detailed manifesto, at the same time a theoretical companion to and a practical training focused on the creation of Beauty.

Theatrical novels

In 1996, when he was awarded the Pushkin Prize, Sokolov briefly—for a single day—returned to Moscow, where he read the essay *An Abstract* to the audience.

While pretending to explain why the author had never written plays, the text is a sort of autobiographical canovaccio:

> when Melpomene [the muse of tragedy] finally smiles upon me I will concoct the hero's fate, concoct and finish playing; it's the theatre of imagination; look and your vision will clear, you'll soar; I will finish playing and writing the text of the play (2012: 75).

Although he never wrote texts intended for theater, Sokolov's novels all contain theatrical motifs and elements. Unsurprisingly, the interwoven structure of pictures and scenes metamorphosing mainly via sound associations, accompanied by the dialogic (or rather monologic) progression of his narrations, has facilitated the adaptation of the books for the stage, beginning with *A School for Fools* (Marchesini 2012b).

The dramatic world is present in Sokolov's books as a recurrent metaphor, a contextual setting or as an intertextual hypotext. Yet a systematic understanding of its role in the writer's poetics is still lacking.

In Sokolov's first novel, there is an authentic, yet peculiar dramatic scene that develops in the middle of the "student so-and-so"'s monologue (or dialogue). This scene imitates a sort of script, including stage directions:

> S. Nikolaev: I will read something else; this is a verse by the Japanese Zen poet Dogen. F. Muromtsev: Zen? That's clear, Semen Danilovich, but you did not give the dates of his birth and death; do so, if it's not a secret. S. Nikolaev: Forgive me, I'll recall them right away, here they are: 1200-1253. Supervisor so-and-so: Only fifty-three years? S. Nikolaev: But what kind of years! F. Muromtsev: What kind? S. Nikolaev, rising from his stool: *In the spring, cherry blossoms, in the summer, the cuckoo. In autumn the moon and in winter the snow, clear and cold.* (Sits down.) That's all (2015: 40).

In the following novel, *Between Dog and Wolf,* the morgue is called an 'Anatomical Theater' inhabited by 'artists' that are presented through their tragic deaths:

> It's time for us, consequently, to get to the *theater*. In the thicket stood, secluded, under the number one, a hunchbacked house. Not really a house but a former chapel with an amputated cross, and some whitish plants, perhaps willows, were bendin over it, like anatomists. And a sign with old-fashioned letters announced: *Anatomical Theater*. A familiarly orderly carried out his duties there. Right away we go to see him in the cellar: Are you keeping watch? Come on, show us your *artists*. The orderly opens the vaults wide: Have a look, I don't mind, so far I don't charge for *shows*. He knew them by histories of their illnesses, with all the details, by heart—who took poison, who burned

from cancer, who got crushed, and who went simply out of stupidity. I remember, he had in storage for about two weeks a gal of *non-advanced age* (2017: 54; italics are mine).

Palisandriia extensively develops the theatrical subtext surrounding the whole world of the Kremlin with a playful, serious-comical aura: "the world of stage, legitimate and otherwise, has supplied the Kremlin with numerous luminaries" (1989: 64). Palisandr himself wears various masks on an existential stage of his own invention:

Gradually my prestige and international reputation grew to unprecedented heights. I became a figure of Rabelaisian proportions, cited and lionized the world over. Suffice it to say that people stopped and stared at P. on the highways and byways of Indonesia and New Zealand, in the valleys of Tibet—and s/he never went out without a mask,

he boldly and confidently states—in the neuter gender in Russian (here rendered as "s/he"), having now discovered his own hermaphrodite nature—, as he approaches the epilogue of his auto-chronicle (1989: 379).

Palisandr's narration even assumes the graphic features of a dramatic script (or a "libretto résumé", as the narrator defines it; 1989: 160) when, for example, he describes, in four acts, a dialogue between himself and Brikabrakov in the second chapter of the novel. The fourth act, restating the musical motif, goes as follows: "Dropping the ax, P. sings his *aria finale*" (1989: 161).

It is also worth noting that, according to past-lover, gerontophile and wannabe historian Palisandr, the present time and its emotions—"the fleeting moment with its pseudo-significance"—are similar to "the ham acting and garish sets of a provincial theatre" (1989: 342).

Finally, the typical situation of metatheater (theater within the theater, best epitomized by *Hamlet*) is also found in *Palisandriia*, in the spectacular scene of the show execution of a fake Beria, of the "symbolic Lavrenty" (1989: 257), which does not lack Shakespearean references:

His thoughts were interrupted by a noise from without, the sound of something banging against something. 'They must be putting up the grandstand,' he said. 'There's a show execution scheduled for tomorrow at two.' 'Not mine, I hope.' 'Oh, no,' he said with an icy smile. 'You'd have been warned in time. It's for the symbolic Lavrenty. [...] You can claim your ticket from the main usher. Your name is on the list.' [...] 'May I have a program?" I asked a passing usher. 'Certainly, sir," he said, handing me one. 'Opera glasses?' '*Merci*, I have my own.' [...] Lavrenty Beria was played by Archibald Hecuba, a major in the entertainment corps. [...] The orchestra struck up the ouverture, and the execution was under way. The victim was pushed to the wall and a hare-skin hood pull over his eyes. The sentence was read in full, the volley fired. 'Shame on the Verbocrucians! Down with the Lord High Aldebaran!' cried the False Lavrenty just before his hands flew up and his body slipped down, clumsily. A few flip-flops and it was all over. The performance was far from successful. Though laconic and finely honed in matters of form, in matters of content it was branded ideologically effete, *decadenza buffa*, all platitude and cliché. [...] 'But hasn't the theatre always been a sacrificial rite? And so I ask, "What's Hecuba to you?"' [...] 'And isn't everything a game anyway? Cards and circuses, billiards and life. You've got to throw yourself into them, play them to the hilt! Think of Hecuba! (1989: 258-260).

Given the particular type of *skaz* employed by Sokolov's first-person narrators, and the deictically prescriptive point of view of these "Perspektiventräger" (Nolting-Hauff 1959: 99), the novels are all fit for the stage in different ways. Referential clarity is dubious. The use of ellipsis and various pragmatic elements with interactive and metatextual function is expanded, complicating the reader's inferential task. The mimesis between textual reality and the reality of the lyric self is total and perfect, so texts almost assume a performative nature, recalling dramatic discourse. The narrator's voice directly defines the narrative "mode" (Segre 1984: 97); there are no mediations. When in *A School for Fools* the voice of the author—in dialogue with his doubled hero—enters the narration, he is but another fictional (and dramatic, one might add) character of the text. The lyric self in Sokolov's novels does not simply respond to Todorov's scheme "Narrateur = Personnage" (1976: 89): such a narrator-character is fundamental in his works due to the fact that he is the one and only real creator of the world into which he forces the reader to enter. So much so that, if in his world paper runs out (as in *A School for Fools*), the novel must suddenly end, in perfect Kharmsian style.

Therefore, it is not difficult to imagine Sokolov's characters on a stage. They are periodically assisted by other contextual figures who are literally born from the flow of their speech. They could also act alone on the scene, though, changing masks and continuing, in a monologic and/or polyphonic manner, their personal and self-referential narration.

Sokolov's "poly-character" (Caramitti 2002: 26) resembles the figure of a Medieval storyteller or a symbolic character: he does not bear a real name (student so-and-so/Nymphaea alba) or has an unstable name (Ilya Zynzyrela bears dozens of variants of his last name, while Palisandr is but a mask-name concealing a hundred thousand faces). This character narrates the world as he interprets it, from his individual and "aberrant" perspective (Simmons 1993: 7), which happens to conflict with the imposed social order.[112] This characteristic has also led critics to speak of *iurodstvo* (Foolishness for Christ) with regard to these narrators (RLJ 1977; Karriker 1979; Johnson 1986b; Simmons 1989; Tumanov 1994; Lipovetsky 1995).

Sokolov, who himself put on a sort of authorial mask after renouncing his first name Aleksandr, seems to share a theatrical conception of life with his characters. After all, in 1996 with the aforementioned essay-monologue *An Abstract*, Sokolov clarified that his life—traced here through a set of stages: from family to friendships and to emigration, the latter seen as the inevitable result of his love for freedom and of his choice to become an "eternal student of the globetrotting department"—is but a play in a "theatre of imagination" (2012: 75). Life, according to Sokolov, is by its very nature a theater; during life, we wear constantly changing masks. Indeed, the Latin etymology of the word *person* is linked to the image of the actor's mask.

Triptych's "theatre of pure reason"

If for Sokolov language and music are closely linked, then possibly the best way to give the word a body is to stage it, to make it resound in all its creative force, evoking figures, images, pictures. In fact, even a simple etymological consideration brings us back to the common ground existing between the poetic and the dramatic word—the act of creating (*poiein*) and the very action (*drama*).

---

[112] Interpretations of Sasha Sokolov's novels as politically engaged texts that denounce the Soviet reality of the time are not convincing. Ludmilla Litus, in particular, reads *A School for Fools* as a text polemically imbued with Soviet reality (1997). However, the novel, although undoubtedly containing references to the Soviet context, does not seem to propose, not even in a veiled form, a political satire; any hint of 'Sovietness' acquires only an aesthetic value for the author. Concentrating on the postmodern aspects of *Palisandriia*, Larissa Rudova, for her part, continues along Litus's line, oversimplifying the reading of Russian postmodernism, which in her view simply "did emerge in response to socialist realism" (2000a). Not only are her arguments in favor of a reading of the novel as an example of *sots-art* unconvincing, but the attempts to read it alternately as a Menippean satire of Bakhtinian definition (albeit with *sots-art* overtones) or as a parodic rewriting of Zamyatin's *We* appear rather forced (2000b, 2006).

The actor himself is, literally, the one who creates, who acts. To create poetry, to create drama is to give voice to a desire and urge of verbal construction. The word acquires a body of its own, being the product of a creative action, whether written or declaimed. In Sokolov's 'theatrical novel' *Triptych*, to quote Bulgakov, the conversing voices—who expressly invite us to read ("to recite"; I: 1) the text out loud—turn into musical instruments interpreting such creation.

Sasha Sokolov himself suggests a dramatic interpretation of his last work, the most theatrical one in his entire oeuvre:

> I cannot boast a great knowledge of theater, but I can well imagine *Triptych* been performed on the stage. A few, or many, actors could interact in the show, or rather all the roles, all the verses could be recited by one actor only. During the act, the actor has to change clothes and masks quickly, so that it is clear who is speaking, otherwise it is not. [...] The three parts that compose *Triptych* can be played one after the other or separately, by single pieces, as it happens in movies, where the action develops through different scenes. It happens so at the cinema or in the classic novel, or in reality, or in dreams. The three parts of this thing are linked by cross-cutting images, not to mention the style, nor the author's point of view on different kinds of past and present phenomena, and being completely silent about the author's feeling and awareness of the chaos and of himself in it.[113]

The discontinuity in the reading, recitation, and dramatic interpretation of *Triptych* reminds Sokolov of cinema and literature, of dreams and reality. In fact, the writer insists that life is not linear at all, it does not proceed according to a logic of cause and effect. Thus, that art which consciously abandons realism (or fictitious naturalism) follows associations and networks of images, motifs, styles, themes.

In this sense *Triptych* does not differ much from the writer's first novel, one also ruled by free associations of sounds and images. In his last literary work, however, the figure of the narrator is blurred, erased, and dissolved in a multitude of ethereal and indefinite voices that do not belong to a single character. This indefinite s/he can therefore be interpreted, according to the writer, by an actor interchanging masks, who stages a sort of polyphonic monologue.

The voices, deprived of distinctive profiles and costumes, claim to be standing on a bare stage in *Triptych*. On this stage, they create everything, including the scenery, through their own speech. Their theater is empty: it has no stages, no

---

[113] Personal communication, email, January 10, 2019.

snack-bar, no props and even no audience. Here, in such a "theatre of pure reason," the audience is not required at all:

> well, come in,
> feel at home or as you wish,
> only don't anticipate the coat-room,
> either coat-room or foyer,
> or snack-bar, or boxes,
> or other outmoded tangibles such as stage or props (III: 20)

> they're absent:
> not needed
> because in the given space
> the performance is not for the public, but exclusively for oneself,
> even more so because the public is also not required (III: 21)

> you lucky dog,
> you found yourself in the institution named after immanuel k,
> in the theatre of pure reason,
> which, inspired, keeps silent all over the *mahashunya* (III: 22)

This theater of silence does not comment on the general *mahashunya*, which in Sanskrit identifies the 'great void' in which every object originates and dissolves. Such is the emptiness of that particular theater in which Sokolov's voices act only for themselves. Playing on the famous expression attributed to Stanislavski "theater begins at the coat-room," they assert that the wardrobe here does not exist. In any case, this is and remains a theater and "theatre, / as every gertrude *[G. Stein is, of course, implied]* knows, / is, exactly, theatre / is, naturally, theatre, / is, indisputably and undeniably, theatre" (III: 19).

For these voices, as well as for the writer, life is by itself theater: in life, we act regardless of the presence of an audience and of the characteristic elements that compose a stage. As a result, the gazebo turns into a "theatre," the conversation into a "drama," and the voices, guided by the stage directions, into a "chorus" reminiscent of the Greek tragedy (II: 11, 12, 13).

Theater itself becomes, as a Discourse, an intertextual motif: the voices rely on its characteristics, forms and elements in order to depict themselves and the reality in which they are immersed. Even stylistically their conversation recalls a script: there are stage directions and other paratextual elements concerning the modalities and the emotional reflections of the speaker ("indifferently," "passionately," "to the side"; II: 12).[114] At the same time, therefore, the voices live and enact a drama on the stage.

In *Philornist*, it is stated that "to fine drama" years now "incline" (an obvious allusion to a verse contained in Pushkin's *Eugene Onegin*). That is why in the flow of the discourse the voices end up talking about characters (that is how the philornist defines himself; III: 7), about roles, parts, actions: "the next installment brings the roles / and parts," "in ensuring / that the filament of the plot is not broken, / and the action, / captivating and educating, / goes on irrepressibly and smoothly" (III: 16, 17). In moving through this drama of our existence, we can only play roles and wear masks.

If life is by itself theater, then the explicit reference to it by the voices in *Triptych* gives rise to metatheater. Such a reflection upon existence unveils the conventionality that the 'stage of life' acquires. However, this theatrical conventionality is not met with dissatisfaction on the part of *Triptych*'s voices, but rather appears as a natural condition of life, which we can forget, but from which we cannot escape:

conventions of various kind are almost invisible (III: 17)

almost,
because not to notice them at all
will not be possible, try as hard as you may,
exactly as it will never be possible
to get rid of them, to reject them,
since it is, after all, theatre (III: 18)

Life is therefore theater, and theater is convention. Consequently, such is life. In contrast to European culture, which, as Mikhail Bakhtin illustrated, has forced popular theater and its 'carnivalesque' to the margins since the 17th century (1965), medieval Japan saw, for example, the birth of Noh theater, which is still represented today on stage. It is not by chance that the voices in *Triptych* mention it (II: 33).

---

[114] The use of non-syntactic gerunds that appear more and more frequently in Sokolov's writing, beginning in particular with *Palisandriia*, relate to this performative task, suggesting ways to imagine specific scenes, acts, dialogues.

On an experimental stage

In order to access this last 'theatrical novel' by Sokolov, it is useful to juxtapose it alongside other productions in the history of theater that have proposed a radical break with traditional forms. In particular, we shall consider the waves of experimentation and research that shook the performative arts in a transversal way in the European continent, from Russia to the Iberian Peninsula, between the end of 19th and the beginning of the 20th centuries, which have influenced contemporary theater.

On the one hand, these artistic attempts rejected the naturalistic drama, and contested the social and moral models of the bourgeoisie. On the other hand, they reacted to the suffocating atmosphere of the time, when the expression of emotions was restricted. New characters were thus introduced to the stage, sometimes appearing more similar to puppets and masks than to individuals. Around the crucial year 1917, the theatrical revolution in Russia contributed to the political and social upheaval, as it intended to erase—at least in words—the old world in order to build a new one.

Moreover, at the time, the success of psychoanalysis favored a new vision of reality as fragmentary and chaotic in its essence, while objective Truth was torn to pieces. On the stage these new ideas took the forms of collage and montage. Finally, technological progress contributed to the overall cultural development, theater included (e.g. the use of electrical lighting on the stage).

In general, the performing arts gradually became detached from the descriptive representation of reality and turned into an ideal place for research on a philosophical or existential level. More precisely, theater became such a space, recovering thus the ancient tradition, that had been progressively relegated to the margins of European bourgeois culture (Bakhtin 1965). To support this perspective, it is useful to look at Meyerhold's "conventional theater" which recovered techniques from the Italian commedia dell'arte. The symbolists also played a key role in the shift from mimetic naturalism to a new poetics of correspondences. Ivanov's 'Tower' represented, in particular, a center of Russian cultural life at the beginning of the 20th century.

At the time, a new theatrical language was being sought that would express the authentic unity between the arts. This wave of experimentation marked an evident divide between the dramatic (literary, written) text and the staging of such texts, conceived as an autonomous and independent artistic activity. Beginning in 1926, as some representatives of Russian formalism moved to Prague, the study of the theatrical text opened up to new analytical perspectives. In the 1930s the first works related to the semiotics of theater appeared (authored by Otakar Zich, Jan Mukařovsky and Pyotr Bogatyrev): their initial assumption was that on the stage every sign undergoes resemantization, thus assuming a new signifier. Upon turning into the 'sign of a sign', the literary text ceases thus to be a simple 'literary text' when it is transposed to the stage. Dialogues, which represent the basis of dramatic texts, do not follow the same laws to which they are subject in literature: "a text, perfectly readable in its literal form, is imperfect for theater" (Canziani 1978: 181), or to quote Bulgakov: "the stage has its own laws" (2007: 120). The dramatic discourse is fundamentally bound to the process of enunciation and to its pragmatic context.

What is, however, valid for mainstream theater, it is not always acceptable to the Avant-Garde. If the traditional dramatic discourse is required to respect a certain coherence—proairetic, referential, discursive, logical, semantic, rhetorical, and stylistic—that guarantees stability, consistency, and constancy (Elam 2005),[115] this same coherence can be broken or challenged by experimental theater. If the pragmatic strategies employed in traditional theater offer the spectator (who does not know the plot) the possibility of understanding and following the development of the action on the stage, experimental theater abolishes the usual automatisms in perception, decoding and comprehension, disrupting the logic of cause and effect, and creating an alienating sensation of absurdity. In the case of *Triptych*, this particular effect of *ostranenie* (defamiliarization) is continuously put into practice by the conversing voices.

Indeed, since the beginning Sokolov's voices are aware that something is not working properly in their composition, or, rather, they know that someone might

---

[115] Elam further explains: "Those objects of discourse which are important components of the dramatic world (e.g. of the *fabula*) must be perceived as stable and consistent entities. Their position, that is, in the dramatic universe of discourse must be coherent rather than capricious (the Caliban referred to is always the same). What guarantees the stability and consistency of the referents is the principle of *co-reference*" (2005: 92-93).

complain about some sloppiness with respect to *fabula* and *siuzhet*. To this concern, they answer:

> but if: perhaps it's exactly the way
> you just announced, but please consider:
> the action of the piece is not developing, it doesn't even have
> a starting point, by neglecting the storyline, you openly
> short-change the plot, then: esteemed gentlemen,
> we are creating here a genuine human document
> and you're bringing up some
> literary tinsel, don't interfere (I: 10)

What the voices are here composing is not some "literary tinsel," but a "genuine human document" for which a precise, pre-established, coherent script is not required: on the stage as much as in life, everything is composed *improptu*, simply here and now.

Triptych's voices are frequently engaged in a metanarrative that is intended to describe the composition itself (a composition about composition). The deictic center, the *origo* to which all of discourses in the book refer to, is precisely this "human document" that is being created "in the virtual continuum" (III: 5) where neither past nor future exist.

Triptych's discourse thus does not meet the logical demands of traditional drama: the lines exchanged between the voices slide one after the other, often disregarding the logic of co-reference in favor of fluid associative networks. If consequentiality in the voices' discourse is erased, however, the main topic remains stable at its center: it is the ongoing creation of Beauty, which is spontaneous, free and uninterrupted, and arises from the insertion of different pictures and episodes in the discourse.

A specific scenario

Scenography is the art (rather than a practice) of creating a third dimension through two-dimensional drawing: it is the big picture in which the theatrical text is inserted. In *Triptych*, the voices sketch this picture with a few rapid lines and modify it from time to time.

It is possible to distinguish a basic (or zero) scenario in contrast to short, contextual scene changes, in which new narrating figures sometimes appear: in these moments, it is as if the stage split, remaining stable on the level of the conversing voices, but renewing itself instead in lateral scenarios. Something similar happens to Palisandr in Sokolov's third novel during the 'stratified' déjà vu he experiences:[116]

> As I ran in from the meadow, where I'd been picking begonias, excited, shedding years with every step, I had one of my attacks of *déjà été*. At this point the author will use an appliqué-like device: he will take the image of my momentary illumination and place it in the perspective of spaces and times (1989: 341).

If in *Discourse* the basic scenario is completely empty (except perhaps for the "to-to" list), the second section's scenario represents a nocturnal gazebo where the voices gather. The *Philornist*'s basic setting is the museum hall where the reader witnesses the Sunday meeting between the "sentinel" and the *señora*. On these basic scenarios, throughout the flow of their speech, the voices 'paint' new "live tableaux" (II: 3).

Thus, when they discuss the value of Latin, they also generate and stage, for example, some short 'Roman' scenes, Latin-like even in their lexical choices:

> and someone who constantly looks at us like a *lupus*,
> this *homo* our mentor *est*,
> but at least the windows of our classroom look out at the coliseum,
> and if saturday comes after all, we hear
> the clinking of armour, roar of animals, screams of the public,
> and, thinking of mucius, we add wings to our minds:
> let them soar (I: 24)

The different scenarios painted by the voices may also host new characters moving within them; the arithmetician and his office, for example, are depicted in the following excerpt:

> so, if you're not busy, here's a tale about one of them,
> who, in modest suspenders and as if nothing were wrong,
> as if he didn't feel that in a short while our comfortable now would ebb away, would pass,
> and another now, foul and unfamiliar, and without special joys, would arrive,
> he bravely serves at the desk of various benefits,
> bravely, but quietly,
> he serves, but isn't servile,

---

[116] In this regard, one may recall the concept of *eonotopos* proposed by Valery Lepakhin in relation to Orthodox iconography: "Events that in reality happened at different times, in the eonotopos can be perceived and depicted as contemporary, since they are within eternity" (2007: 149).

and doesn't make too much of himself or of his courage,
only occasionally he remembers and smiles in his heart:
i am an arithmetician (II: 30)

The *señora* who, in the end, interacts with the museum "sentinel," observes the vow of silence: the philornist wonders whether that is because she lost her husband in war. The flow of the discourse turns the museum into a new setting, as these veterans are depicted now "feathered":

[they], in essence, returned,
but were chased away,
since they were not recognized (III: 52)

'cause they appeared with different features,
resembling heavenly byrds [...] (III: 53)

and they flew away not to return anymore,
and remembering them,
people said they died the death of the quite valiant [...] (III: 54)

looking at the manuscript,
the crowned censor,
considered the best stylist of the fatherland,
made a note on the margin: *style*,
and was so gracious
he offered right there his own variant:
they died the death of the fine (III: 55)

Leaving the silent lady in the museum, the reader is introduced to wars and battlefields, then to the reappearance of those killed, now transformed into "heavenly byrds." From the description of their death, and through the manuscript, we are reminded of the significance of the thematization of writing and of finesse (*iziashchnoe*) in general, that creation of Beauty that binds everything in *Triptych*. One scene bleeds into another, from which yet another arises; they are like Chinese boxes (or a matryoshka doll[117]), one preserved inside the other.

---

[117] This is exactly how Palisandr described his multivolume memoirs: "One might say it is constructed according to the *matryoshka*, or Russian doll, principle: a novel within a novel within a novel *und so weiter*"—the *matryoshka* being, according to his definition, "an optimistic tragedy about reincarnation, about karma, about conception; it is a charming human comedy coated with a healthy layer of the gloss Russians are so well known for"

The book's final scenario is the nocturnal Venetian lagoon. As the *señora* turns into a heron and the philornist dissolves, the conversing voices reappear (perhaps the philornist has transformed into them). In their discussion they recall an evening in Venice. The scene is lit up by the precarious flame of a match, or by fireworks that are continuously extinguished, thereby suggesting a finale completely shrouded in darkness: the voices leave the stage and enter a *trattoria*, while their companion-gondolier goes back to his island-cemetery.

In *Triptych*, lights and shadows, which represent essential elements on the stage, are not only mentioned in the final scene, or during the starry night spent by the voices under the gazebo. The arithmetician, for example, is said to leave his office last every day, turning off the lights; only the outside lamp remains lit, "extract[ing] the entrance door from the darkness" (II: 32). This light is noticed by a passer-by who was "perhaps [...] the best gaffer in the theater *noh*," and who, "admiring the cinder of a chinese match," experienced the sudden awakening of the *dunwu* (II: 33). The battle-concert that results in the officer-violinist's death takes place as the fog dissolves, in what would be complete darkness if not for the moonlight (II: 73). In short, on *Triptych*'s stage the scene blurs light and darkness, one quickly turning into the other. In these scenarios the passage between the two is clear, marked by the definitive burning of a match, or by the sudden disappearance of the fog.

In dark contexts, the light generates a warm aura, revealing the landscape's profiles and outlines. Nevertheless, this light does not illuminate the scene completely, as it is an ephemeral source, destined to be extinguished in complete darkness, as in the finale, or to merge into the beginning of the day, as in the last stanzas of *Gazebo*. In fact, according to Scandello's words, it is not in nocturnal gardens that Beauty shall be created, but more precisely in "pre-dawn ones" (II: 5), that is to say in the morning twilight (*utrennie sumerki*). The twilight praised by Scandello is yet another literary embodiment of those *sumerki* that represent a poetic dominant in Sokolov's imagery and, as Mario Caramitti explains, they are the "programmatic mirror of Sokolov's metamorphic and multi-layered universe" (2019: 424).

(1989: 308). Once again, Palisandr refers back to the world of theater, the favorite intertextual context for this graphomaniac protagonist.

The theatrical motif that runs through Sasha Sokolov's latest work therefore takes on two forms: on the one hand, it is expressly related to the metanarrative; on the other, it permits a figurative, visual concretization of *Triptych*'s verbal music. In the first case, the text encompasses explicit references to the stage, to the scene and its characteristics. In the second case, the voices' conversation continuously evokes theatrical associations through the word, images and new scenarios.

The theatrical motif also reflects Sokolov's poetics and take on artistic creation. The twilight atmosphere, erosion of the plot, linguistic research, and the circular conception of time make *Triptych* the most mature and coherent metamorphosis of Sokolov's novels, but with a new skin. *Triptych* approaches the idea of total art, disavowing barriers and inviting all disciplines, ideas, and objects to take part in the authentic creation of Beauty.

The aim of this investigation was to assess the role that language plays in Sasha Sokolov's oeuvre and to understand the way it works according to the writer's poetics. Although critics have frequently observed the idiosyncratic use of Russian employed in Sokolov's texts and the resulting difficulties encountered in reading and translation, a systematic investigation of Sokolov's linguistic game has been lacking.

This chapter has identified the authorial theoretical framework within which language is mastered in the texts. Drawing on previous research, this analysis has shown that the word, made sacred through its evocative and ontological power, engages phonetically in a particular type of musical composition. Music, being intertextually and metaphorically present in all of Sokolov's texts, enters the writer's cosmos since the writing process reproduces the work of a composer. Sokolov's texts can thus be interpreted as verbal musical compositions.

Consequently, these works require a perfect sense of hearing and a proper knowledge of their sound alphabet. This is why, on the other hand, the chapter has explored the results of Sasha Sokolov's word weaving: if music is the artistic field to which this writing activity relates, a proper performance is needed to truly appreciate it. Sokolov's texts instinctively suggest what in Russian is defined as *ispolnenie*, literally the fulfillment of the form, which acquires its own body, an actual (vocal) concretization. The stage is thus a natural element in Sokolov's cosmos: besides having been repeatedly adapted for theater, his books contain elements related to the world of drama. Additionally, Sokolov's narrators—the voices that guide the reader (or listener) through the pages—may well be imagined as if performing on a stage.

The combination of musical and performative aspects in Sasha Sokolov's writing is among the most significant findings emerging from this study. The exploration, based on concrete textual evidence, complements the results of earlier analyses. In particular, concentrating on Sokolov's last published and less studied work *Triptych*, the present chapter includes compelling insights that offer a better understanding of this recent text while situating it in the broader panorama of Sokolov's works.

The present investigation has significant implications for understanding of the poetics of one of the most prominent authors of Russian contemporary literature. This contribution, also in the light of the interpretation of the notion of *proeziia* explored in the following chapter, constitutes the first comprehensive assessment of the authorial theoretical framework and of the expressive effects achieved by Sasha Sokolov in his literary activity. Moreover, this is the largest study so far enhancing the understanding of *Triptych*.

Chapter 4.
Theory and Play of *Proeziia*

> "Do love painting, poets!"
> Nikolay Zabolotsky, *Portrait*

In 1989, during his stay in the Soviet Union, Sasha Sokolov released an interview to Ivan Podshivalov, journalist at the "Moskovskii komsomolets". An abridged English translation of their conversation later appeared in the 2006 issue of "Canadian-American Slavic Studies" devoted to Sokolov's work. This publication was integral to this second monographic issue of the journal, as it contains the first authentic definition of Sokolov's key word 'proeziia'.

> IVAN PODSHIVALOV: Do you identify the genre of your works in any way?
> SASHA SOKOLOV: No, not really, but it seems to me that they are not novels in the conventional sense. In the West, it was and perhaps still is fashionable among avant-garde writers not to identify a work's genre and to call it simply "text." Sometimes, I also do that. This is something peculiar to contemporary literature. Genre boundaries have eroded, and there is no need to reestablish them. The time has come for a new period of synthesis. As I explained, genre interests me less than the kinds of works I write. I create *proetry* (*proezia*). This term is my discovery. Although, of course, I am far from being the first, and, more likely, I am the last in a long line of followers of the tradition that includes Turgenev and Bunin. Earlier, there were verses in prose, yet it remained prose. I think of myself as a *proet*. For some reason, no one has hit on this term earlier, although it lies right there on the surface (Podshivalov 2006: 352).

In the same year, Sokolov published his essay *The Shared Notebook or a Group Portrait of SMOG*—the only text he could officially publish directly in the USSR. In this essay, he again emphasizes that he is a *proet*:

> Aren't you a poet, by chance? A move. I am a *proet*. A move. Pro what, sir? A move. Pro such things as a morning and evening twilight, a raven and a turtle dove, hail and rain, and a young female Gipsy dancer with castanets in the thicket of the sandalwood grove for whom we lose everything but our sandals: ringy-dingy. A *proet* is—if you will—a bastard, a mixture of prose writer and lyricist, half this and half that. But what the rascal produces—is *proeziia* of blue blood and pure tears. Basically, tears of amazement, which, when taken in the major scale, back-to-front, or with the inner side of the hide facing outside—must be called endearment. It is the *proeziia* of unobstructed amazism, here, amid the ugliness of this world (2012: 49).

This extremely musical and hermetic essay is a perfect example of the "*proeziia* of blue blood and pure tears," a "*proeziia* of the best amazism"—in

Russian, *izumizm*, a term coined by Sokolov's fellow *smogist* Leonid Gubanov (from *izumit'*, to astonish, surprise), universally recognized as the poet-genius of the SMOG group.[118]

In this text, Sokolov not only outlines the concept of *proeziia*, but he also transforms *The Shared Notebook* into a *proetic* manifesto of *proeziia* by lyrically blending form and content.

The aim of this chapter is to explore the implications of Sokolov's adherence to *proeziia*, to analyze and expound what this term means, and to argue that it identifies a specific macro-genre that fits appropriately into Sokolov's baroque poetics.

A long *proetic* tradition

As Sasha Sokolov himself acknowledges, he is far from being the first acolyte of the synthetic literary lineage he defines as 'proeziia'. The author, conscious of his own literary roots, has never made a secret of his favorite readings, especially among Russian classics. Sasha Sokolov has often characterized himself as an heir to the Russian literary tradition, closely associating himself with Pushkin and Gogol, among others. In an interview with Olga Matich, he affirmed: "Pushkin is dear to me first and foremost as a person. [...] Gogol [...] is close to me only as a writer" (Matich 1985a: 12). Moreover, intertextuality as a recurrent element in Sokolov's texts helps to identify the texts that have most influenced Sokolov.

However, Sokolov's inheritance from the Russian literary tradition extends beyond themes and stylistic features. More importantly, he has inherited a specific attitude towards the text and its creation: he belongs to the traditional Russian category of the 'writer-theorist' who reflects deeply on the meaning and properties of literary genres.

The question of genre has long represented a central issue within European literature, at least since the epoch of Classicism and the Romantic Revolution. Intolerant of being pigeonholed into strict categories, writers in Russia have challenged the norms of genre, renewed them, and questioned epic, lyric, and

---

[118] Aleinikov wrote of Gubanov: "He was tirelessly amazed at his own talent and not infrequently amazed others with it, with his ardent, creative, extraordinary play and intellect" (1989: 81-82). On Gubanov's *izumizm*, see also Krokhin (1992: 100-103).

novelistic models. Each Russian literary masterpiece has opened and closed its own genre, at the same time grafting itself into the great "system of literature" and becoming part of the tradition (Tynyanov 1929). The novel in particular is the genre most open to renewal and reworking, as Mikhail Bakhtin underlined in his studies (1975).

From Pushkin to Tolstoy to Pasternak, experimentation—if it can be called 'experimentation' at all, given the constancy and regularity of the phenomenon—concerned not only the categories of genre, style, and subject, but also often translated into 'paratextual' dissonance. That is to say, it was typical of many nineteenth-century works—and not only if we consider, for example, Yerofeyev's 'poem' *From Moscow to Petushki*—for the author to include a descriptive subtitle informing the reader of the text's genre. However, since the creation of the 'novel in verse' *Eugene Onegin*, Russian audiences have become accustomed to considering genres as fluid, rather than fixed categories and accepting the use of non-normative subtitles and classificatory techniques.

Such a practice simultaneously underscores the interdependency of literary theory and practice in the work of these 'writer-theorists' (or 'writer-philosophers', as in the case of Tolstoy). The use of defamiliarizing subtitles—besides Pushkin's 'novel in verse', the 'poems' of Gogol or Dostoevsky may serve as further examples—demonstrates that respect for the canon in the strictly normative sense was perceived as a limitation in Russia. Conversely, an open approach to the canon—an 'anti-canonical' approach—proved to be more fruitful and stimulating. In other words, poets and writers have always known that, as Tynyanov put it, there are no ready-made literary genres and genre designations are given only *a posteriori* and in relation to the specific system of literature. The ode of Afanasy Fet is, as the formalist critic wrote, not the ode of Lomonosov's time. Only in the European genre system are prose and poetry distinguished mainly on a stylistic basis—thus metrical prose is called 'prose', while the *vers libre* (even when deprived of a metrical scheme) is considered 'poetry' (Tynyanov 1929).

To return to the theme of Sokolov's *proeziia*, Russian literary tradition has provided readers with a number of representative predecessors—for example, Turgenev and Bunin, to quote Sokolov. Perhaps more significantly, it has defined the orientation of writers in relation to the literary canon by inviting them to reflect personally on literary activity and to concretize their views in original creations, thereby questioning and renewing the canon.

In his own reflection, Sokolov noted the inadequacy of canons, the arbitrariness of rules and conventions in art, while emphasizing that authentic masterpieces cannot be limited or defined by these rules. Some of these masterpieces have become an indelible, deeply rooted part of the European-Christian tradition, although they often seem to go unnoticed.

Along these lines, Sokolov has lamented that among the great masterpieces commonly cited by critics, one is usually left without due attention, even though it is perhaps the most important artistic model: the Bible, which does not conform to a particular canon, a genre, a well-defined tradition. Like any great book, the Bible forms a genre unto itself.

> I always felt that in this list [of masterpieces] the best books were really missing—clearly the Bible, the New Testament. How much did the authors of the New Testament write? Somebody 20 pages, somebody else 40, and that's it. That's how much it takes to write. You cannot get a single word out of that. The misfortune of prose seems to me to be that 90% of the words are completely superfluous. [...] I grew up in a Christian country, in the Holy Rus. I simply had no other choice, I was shaped as a Christian. I do not go to church, yet I feel that I think according to Christian categories. And that was absolutely natural when I started reading the New Testament. It all fell into place: this is my relationship to reality. This is how one should live, I thought while reading the Gospel (Kochetkova 2017).

Sokolov regrets that although the literary beauty of the Bible is undeniable, it is often forgotten. Its aesthetic qualities are often subordinated to the text's religious interpretation. Many Biblical verses, very short and 'condensed', have been forever etched into the cultural memory of the Christian world: these verses are unsurpassed in form and content thanks to the timeless finesse of their *proeziia*. Indeed, Sokolov would likely classify the textual typology of the Bible as *proeziia*.[119]

In studying Biblical rhetoric, Roland Meynet found that repetition is its predominant figure, while binarity and parataxis (repetitive structures at the syntactic level) are its essential features (2012). Not surprisingly, according to

---

[119] "We can say that a whole series of biblical texts are nothing but *proeziia*, but we would surely have a lot of opponents" (Personal communication, email, August 08, 2019).

Jakobson (1990), parallelism and repetition are among the stylistic devices underlying poetry since its beginnings.

The fact that prior to the 17th century Russian culture did not know any distinction between texts in verse and texts in prose, but only recognized a division between sung and spoken texts, naturally affected the development of literature. The blurred lines between prose and verse (*stikh*)—and not between prose and poetry (*poeziia*)[120]—have interested both writers and critics. This relationship affects not only the organization of the text, but also the epistemological categories of linearity, causality, objectivity (Albanese 2017: 4-5). This process of 'contamination' generates hybrid results including, but not limited to, *montazhnye teksty*, prosimetra, the *udeteron* (literally, 'neither this nor that', neither poetry nor prose), the *monostikh* (one-line poem), metrical and rhythmic prose, Turgenev's 'prose poems', or what Gasparov defined as *mnimaia proza,* 'mock prose' (1993).[121]

In general, these stylistic hybridizations are primarily based on the author's intention and "orientation" (as Yuri Orlitsky defines it, 2002) towards the prosaic or poetic model. The graphic organization of the discourse results from the author's inclination.

The poet and critic Artyom Skvortsov recently contended that it is appropriate to apply the analytical criteria with which one generally approaches poets to a number of Russian prose writers (2018). Skvortsov names Gogol as the progenitor of these 'prose-poets', who unsurprisingly looked to Dante's *Comedy* for his masterpiece. Gogol was then followed by a long line of authors: from Remizov to Bely, from Babel to Olesha, in addition to Mariengof and Vaginov, to Zhitkov, Krzhizhanovsky and Platonov, to end with Nabokov, Valentin Kataev, Venedikt Yerofeyev, and Yuri Koval. Sasha Sokolov, Skvortsov claims, is a member of the last generation of these poets *incognito*, along with Tolstaya, Eppel, Shishkin, Gol'dshtein.

---

[120] The Russian terms *poeziia* and *stikhi* are not synonymous: the *stikh* refers to the actual architecture of the text, while *poeziia* in a broader sense considers the internal structure of a text in its interconnection of various expressive elements. Sasha Sokolov in his theorization of *proeziia* is aware of the fact that poetry and prose are not antonyms.

[121] On this topic, see Yuri Orlitsky's studies (1991, 2002, 2008).

Skvortsov's article also provides the tools to identify a 'prose-poet'. Their prose is marked by the primacy of style over plot; the interest in language, figures of speech, sound, puns; the metricalization of the text; the sound/phonic harmony; the poetic syntax; the self-sufficiency of images and the high degree of metaphoricity and pictoriality, which impede the understanding of the text and lead to a careful reading; the reduction (or complete absence) of dialogue between characters, which is replaced by semi-free or indirect speech; the reduction of narrative tension to the point of erasing the entire plot; the development of the narrative through associations of ideas, sounds, and images. Skvortsov notes that "certainly the features enumerated here may be present in any prose work in different ways, but their common presence, their critical weight, clearly testifies to the fact that something in this prose does not function normally" (2018). In some cases, it is also important to pay attention to the biography of the author: often, these are writers who first debuted as poets or who wrote both poetry and prose.

Skvortsov chose a line from Sokolov's *Triptych* as the title for this article: *Appeared with different features* (III: 53), referencing the hybrid nature of 'prose-poets'. In *Triptych*, those who appear with different features—namely, winged, halfway between angels and birds—are not recognized by their wives and mothers and are therefore chased away. Skvortsov comments:

> Here we are talking about those poets who appear to readers with different features and are therefore often predestined to remain unrecognized and misunderstood. Yet these creators emerge from time to time, and their aim is to raise prose to the heights of poetry (2018).

It is precisely the adoption of a non-prescriptive point of view that allows us to better grasp Sokolov's elusive *proetic* work.

A choice of awareness

In his 1989 interview with Ivan Podshivalov, Sokolov suggested that "the time has come for a new period of synthesis," explaining the widespread tendency to refer to a literary work simply as a "text"—a choice he himself made in 1977 when he titled *Tekst,* a first excerpt from *Between Dog and Wolf* published in the pages of "Glagol" (1977: 7-24). In the deeply meta-narrative *Triptych*[122] Sokolov reemphasized this point, suggesting that the text be called a "thing," "since every composition can be called simply a thing" (II: 65).[123]

This is a clear rejection of traditional definitions of genres, opening the possibility for both author and reader to move freely not only between poetry and prose (and the choice to cite Dante's *Vita nuova* in II: 76, a prosimetrum par excellence, does not seem accidental), but more generally between the arts, broadly defined. In *Triptych*, the dialoguing voices assert that even arithmetic, biology and philosophy are also arts in their own way, since they are means to (re)create Beauty and to meditate on it. In a Babelic and ecumenical embrace of universal knowledge, the author suggests the elimination of the barriers between fields of knowledge, between languages (living or extinct), and alphabets.

It seems to be no coincidence that "Veshch'" (Thing) was the name of the magazine founded in Berlin in 1922 by El Lissitzky and Ilya Ehrenburg, whose slogan was "Art is now international" (*Iskusstvo nyne internazional'no*).[124] The idea—not new to the Russian world[125]—was to unite the world's (or at least the European) representatives of the Avant-Garde, from painting to cinema, from music to theater. Art, as interpreted by these intellectuals and as affirmed in Sokolov's *Triptych*, exists only as a series of fluid and interrelated elements that influence and overlap: art is inherently indivisible.

Sokolov is thus aware of the long tradition of artists who aimed to overcome arbitrary distinctions in art and to blend genres and literary-artistic traditions. Nevertheless, there is a crucial difference in that he insists that he himself established the birth of a new literary lineage, which he calls *proeziia*. This

---

[122] The continuous commentary on the text in parallel with the development of the discourse guides the reading and makes clear what may seem obscure at first glance.
[123] It should also be noted that, even in interviews, Sokolov does not disdain the use of the term "thing" to describe his own and others' works (Personal communications, email, December 17, 2017; January 10, 2019; July 03, 2019; July 10, 2019).
[124] The working languages of this magazine were German, French, and Russian.
[125] For example, the magazine "Mir iskusstva", founded by Sergei Diaghilev in 1899, aimed to break down the boundaries between the arts in order to create a universal art that knew no division between the Western and Eastern worlds. On the relations between El Lissitzky, Kazimir Malevich and the concept of 'total art', see also the studies of Boris Groys, such as *Utopiia i real'nost'* (2013).

difference lies in the fact that Sokolov is fully aware of the nature of his own writing due to his personal theoretical reflection on his own work and lyrical chords. Sokolov is not so much interested in the genre label as he is in the freedom to cross boundaries and incorporate aspects from any literary tradition, whether it is poetic or prosaic.

To be a *proet* means to consciously elevate oneself above sterile debates and taxonomic definitions, to abandon arbitrary and preconceived canons. Through his theorization of *proeziia*, Sokolov seems to be responding in his own way to the critics' need to categorize the works and authors they approach: if it is absolutely necessary to define a genre in accordance with the rules of literary analysis, then Sokolov's will be hybrid and of his own invention.

A baroque macro-genre

It is not enough, however, to simply state that Sokolov's attitude to literary creation and his deliberate avoidance of strict and arbitrary rules justifies the birth of a vague literary 'thing' called *proeziia*. The dissimulative character typical of this writer conceals his profound and thoughtful reflection on the subject; it is clear, though, that Sokolov's very insistence on his coining the term and identifying his work with it bears witness to the importance that *proeziia* has acquired in the eyes of this writer. The aim of this section is to define *proeziia* and situate it within the author's own theory of literary creation by highlighting the features that make it suitable and appropriate for what was described, in Chapter 2, as a specific 'Sokolovian baroqueness'.

In addition to Vail' and Genis's definition of Baroque (1980), which they used to identify the 'Soviet baroque', a number of other characteristics will be mentioned here to define this seventeenth-century artistic sensibility.

In architecture, the concatenated use of formally heterogeneous volumes and geometries and the interactive incorporation of light and volume were emphasized to create new spatial concepts. Spectacular designs and complex illusions were combined with the artist's imagination and addressed to the viewer with a specific rhetoric of emotional persuasion. The interaction and fusion of the various arts became the norm and guaranteed the development of new spatial structures.

In literature, novelty and sophistication acquired a predominant role. They were realized through witty combinations of heterogeneous images, through an amalgamation of distant notions based on secret and subtle connections and analogies that the artist's intellect perceived and detected in every natural phenomenon (the language of nature, of animals and plants, of God). Another technique was the reworking of clichés and figurative expressions in unexpected ways imbued with new meanings.

In the baroque sensibility, authentic aesthetic pleasure emerged from these witty intellectual exercises. As a result, in subsequent centuries, the Baroque assumed the status of a vain pastime, an aberration of aesthetic taste.

If the Renaissance valorized the metaphor and the epigram, the Baroque made word and image work together, reinforcing the former with additional visual representations (visual poetry). Indeed, the scientific revolution shattered previously accepted truths and ushered in an era of anxiety: artists and intellectuals turned to research and experimentation, opened themselves to free and innovative forms, and discovered in nature the myriad anomalies, exceptions, as well as the metamorphic essence of the world. The baroque eye investigated areas that had not been surveyed, explored the network of natural connections, and proposed a new map of the world suggesting how to navigate it.

As argued in Chapter 2, Sasha Sokolov's poetics cannot be fully and uncritically attributed to seventeenth-century baroque aesthetics. Certainly, however, a number of the above features can be traced in his work, but they are reworked to compose the author's poetics, which can be loosely defined as 'Sokolovian baroqueness'. The concept of *proeziia* is a new and elaborated definition of a specific literary sensibility.

Proeziia—a concept never systematically defined by its author, but extensively developed in his work—is a term Sokolov uses in order to identify his own work independently of canonical labels. In the essay *The Shared Notebook*, it is suggested that this term represents the result of the sophisticated mixture of an author's lyrical and prosaic 'orientations'. *Proeziia*, in this sense, is a 'vessel' that accommodates within itself a variety of artistic concretizations, excluding none. *Proeziia* best encompasses the features of Sasha Sokolov's literary work—the multi-layered structure of networks linked by schemes of repetition and variation, the erasure of boundaries and limits, the multiplication of possibilities of artistic creation and interpretation, its spiraling process of encoding and decoding. Thanks to its open and undefined nature, this 'vessel' aptly accommodates this set of formal and content-related features. Form and content, loosely defined, influence each other like communicating vessels.

At first, one might assume that *proeziia* denotes a kind of genre label that can be applied to Sokolov's texts. On this basis, some critics have indeed identified some parallels between Sokolov's *proeziia* and, in particular, the tradition of *menippea* or *burlesque* literature, both genres that belong (also) to the seventeenth-century sensibility and aesthetics (Salomatin, Skvortsov 2021).[126] But this definition is problematic: not only would it directly contradict the author's intention to erase the very notion of genre and canon (and thus establish a new, *proetic* genre), but it would also render meaningless Sokolov's proposal to interpret *Triptych* as a "proem" (*proema* in Russian)[127]—if "proem" is the genre of *Triptych*, then what is *proeziia*?

More than his three novels, examples of *proeziia* are represented mainly by Sokolov's essays (notably, *The Anxious Pupa* and *The Shared Notebook*, the latter being a kind of practical guide to *proetic* writing) and, according to Boguslawski (2012), Kislov (2012), Gulin (2012), by *Triptych* too. For Gulin this last book is a kind of "programmatic realization" (*programmnoe osushchestvlenie*) of the term, while for Boguslawski *Gazebo* is "perhaps the best example of *proeziia* created by the author to date" (2012: xvii).

However, given the 'vertical' organization of the text, it seems inappropriate to refer to *Triptych* by this term, as Sokolov himself notes: "As far as I understand

---

[126] In this article, the two Russian critics summarize Sokolov's main features as follows: "play and burlesque" (*igra i burlesk*), "menippeanity" (*menippeinost'*), "proeziia", "laughter principle" (*smekhovoe nachalo*). The theoretical influence of Mikhail Bakhtin's work is obvious. Salomatin and Skvortsov also trace some innovative parallels between Sokolov's and Oleg Chukhontsev's poetics: the latter "arrived at remarkably similar typological results out of personal explorations. [...] What we observe here is not a borrowing, but a typological convergence of original masters of the word on a parallel path, for whom centuries-old layers of menippea, burlesque, play and laughter culture were equally important."

[127] "Possibly, we can approach *Triptych* in many different ways: it can be seen as a three-part *proem*, or as a mini-novel, or as an abstract of a novel, or as three plays for several voices" (Personal communication, email, January 10, 2019).

it, *Tryptich* is written in vers libre, but if we were to display this text horizontally, we would get *proeziia*."[128]

What do Sokolov's essays and *Triptych* have in common, given their differences in terms of text organization, content, and stylistic features? Fundamentally, these works all present an obvious rhythmic structure, although on a comparative level of analysis, no specific meter prevails. Sokolov is a connoisseur of prosody studies,[129] and if he had intended to establish a fixed metrical pattern for his *proetic* invention, he would indeed have made it explicit. *Proeziia*, however, must be something other than (or at least more than) a 'mere' adoption of a rhythmic prose model, of which there are numerous examples in the history of literature.

I would argue, then, that Sasha Sokolov's *proeziia* should be interpreted as a macro-genre describing a form of 'horizontal' literary writing whose compositional structure is based, more than on strict formal rules, on a harmonic (musical) criterion. This compositional structure refers to sounds and words as connecting links in a chain of interwoven associations that develop through layers of spiraling multiplications—all features that fit into the 'Sokolovian baroqueness'.

Defined as a macro-genre, Sokolov's *proeziia* describes a literary text that is the result of a composition that is at once verbal and musical. Such a composition fluidly flows like notes on a staff—hence 'horizontally' from a graphic point of view, and yet 'vertically' in a performative sense, as the printed notes receive their concrete realization when played or sung—according to their natural value (duration), pitch, loudness, and timbre.

The beauty of a literary text, as implied by Sokolov's conceptualization of *proeziia*, derives from its natural and fluid organization, free from external constraints. The intrinsic harmony of the universe is meant to be read and heard

---

[128] Ibidem.

[129] For example, when asked to compare *Triptych*'s first lines with Brodsky's poem *From Nowhere with Love*, Sokolov goes into detail, demonstrating a perfect awareness of and attention to notions of rhythm inscribed in a syllable-tonic framework: "Brodsky's line features fourteen syllables, mine twelve. His stressed syllables are the third, sixth, eighth, fourteenth. My stressed syllables are the fourth, seventh, twelfth. His caesura comes after the seventh syllable. Mine after the fourth" (Personal communication, email, July 10, 2019).

and then, if one wills, transcribed to our best abilities. The result, if successful, will be *proeziia*.

In Lieu of a Conclusion

In the essay *The Key Word of Belles-Lettres*, Sasha Sokolov maintains that, over the course of a day, there is often just enough time to read a book's first phrases before sleeping:

> Obviously, this is better than nothing. Particularly when one recalls what importance the classics ascribe to the first sentence. Hemingway used to say that the fate of the rest of the work depends on it. [...] My principle is that the first chord of prose should sound like the first line of a poem. [...] To prove that I am right, compare the brilliance of each of those phrases with the brilliance of the first line of the Holy Bible: 'In the beginning God created the heavens and the earth.' In the meantime I will compare the first phrase of a prose work with a note, played by a tuner on a pitch pipe or with a symbolic key that sets the tone of the following music. The first phrase can be called a verbal key to the fortress of form. It is the key that answers the question: by what means? It is the key in the shape of a short word *how* (2012: 26-27).

First sentences indeed play a central role in Sokolov's work, as they assume a performative character: the "student so-and-so" wonders "how to begin, with what words"; while stylizing the epistolary genre Ilya Zynzyrela says to his addressee, "with Your permission, I commence"; *Palisandriia*'s opening note "From the Biographer" inserts the narrative into an epic frame, preparing the reader for what he is about to encounter; *Triptych* opens again, like the first novel, as if *in medias res*, and again the narrating voices stress the importance of carefully researching the right words—or, as Sokolov might put it, the right "note." However, his latest work engages with this eternal dilemma: "*tipa togó*" (of the kind that), says the voice emerging in the first line of the first stanza, as if to mean: first let us say something beautiful, and the content will fit the form; if the form is in place, then the content will follow.

Closing sentences in Sokolov's work raise a similar problem. His novels may end due to external causes (the Author runs out of paper in *A School for Fools*); or they take on a performative (almost theatrical) significance—Ilya ironically signs his letter ("And the signature, if I may. And those who are illiterate—a cross. [...] All the most exceptional to You"; 2017: 200) and the Binging Hunter menaces "I dare you to burn, you dumb-as-a-bell, / My amazing, ingenious lines!" (2017: 230); Palisandr triumphantly returns to Russia; *Triptych*'s closing *arrivederci* greeting promises new encounters. Such endings fail to put an actual end to the narrative, which could continue, or start once again from the beginning.

This conclusion will similarly fail to put an authentic end to the analysis of the literary work (and world) of Sasha Sokolov: the topics the four chapters have touched upon could be usefully explored in further research. Moreover, having once surprised his readers and passionate critics with the unexpected publication of *Triptych*, we should not exclude some new moves from Sokolov himself. To date, however, we shall interpret *Triptych* as his last complete book and, therefore, as his ultimate poetic manifesto that has come after a lifetime of personal research on the creative power of the word—a life that Chapter 1 investigates, touching upon both biographical steps and artistic results and goals. *Triptych* has reshuffled and condensed all those features that were previously scattered in Sokolov's novels and essays, providing critics with some new analytical tools and readers with tips on how to extrapolate useful keys to understanding his entire oeuvre.

In this last work, which came more than twenty years after the publication of Sokolov's third novel, the author gathered what he sowed over a period of more than thirty years, resuming discourses, motives, images, expressions, concepts concerning art and reality: although "with different features" (III: 53), the writer continued to write the very same text, remaining faithful to his research around the *kak*, his ideal 'how'. Chapter 2 summarizes the analytical work advanced so far by critics, culminating with new investigations concerning *Triptych*, and exploring the elements that compose Sokolov's literary (and rather baroque) cosmos.

Sound and image, key to his previous work, are doubly essential in *Triptych*: the entire structure of the text rests on their bond, which completely supplants the role of plot. *Triptych*'s unifying theme is the creation of Beauty, of 'finesse' (*iziashchnoe*), which results from the unity of the arts. The *proet* is that artist who realizes the creative synthesis, recognizing the indissoluble artistic triangle formed by word, sound, and body—an idea explored in depth in Chapter 3, which touches upon the idiosyncratic linguistic practice employed by Sasha Sokolov, its background and results. The widespread presence of theatrical references in Sokolov's texts and the writer's own statements about a possible adaptation of *Triptych* for the stage suggest (at least hypothetically) the possibility of a performative representation, whether spoken or sung. As the Russian term *ispolnenie* suggests, such a representation would 'fill' the form, would materially, bodily concretize it.

Music and theater are not the only disciplines mentioned in *Triptych*: the voices talk about various fields of knowledge, loosely borrowing their specific terminology, sometimes modifying it, or creating neologisms. Among these fields, the reader encounters astronomy, mathematics, philosophy, and Eastern doctrines and cultures. It is interesting to note that Schopenhauer—the Western philosopher who was closest to and borrowed the most from Eastern philosophies—considered music as the supreme form of art, thus echoing the "failed composer" Sokolov.

The writer often employs images and terminology derived from fields of knowledge that individually endeavor to offer the most universal and harmonious interpretation of reality, of the universe, of life. Through a totalizing and harmonious embrace, Sokolov is able to seek and create 'finesse' starting from the heterogeneity of the world.

Language serves as the verbal—but, at the same time, musical and pictorial—instrument of this exploration. Language is allowed to use foreign words and expressions, as well as to modify them and create new ones in order to better suit the demands of Beauty. Thus, Sokolov's *proetic* language is the result of an indissoluble interweaving of several languages in a nourishing Russian (and Old Russian) broth—in a way, it is reminiscent of Zamenhof's Esperanto and of Comenius's *panglossia*, which gathered from existing languages the constitutive elements—grammatical, morphological, syntactic, lexical—of an idiom that would overcome the hegemony of certain languages and thus offer a truly universal language.[130] Sokolov seems to have reiterated since, at least, his English "nightingale" appearing in *A School for Fools*, that if "everything in the world is connected" (I: 46), so too must be languages.

The voices in *Triptych* speak several languages and freely interweave topics and images, guiding the reader and intratextually commenting on the literary

---

[130] The pedagogical reform dreamed by the Bohemian philosopher in his *Via lucis* (1668) envisioned the establishment of a *pansophic* state utopia. *Panglossia* would have served as its official language, thus overcoming the political and structural limits of Latin.

creation at work. They are immersed in an ethereal dimension of non-time and non-place: they are anyone, anywhere, at any time—all possible space-time circumstances are here merged. In this virtual eternity, everything is bound together and destined to reoccur, as happened in *Between Dog and Wolf*'s and, especially, in *Palisandriia*'s *bezvremen'e* which starts after Beria commits suicide by hanging himself on the Kremlin tower clock at 8.44 (exactly when the hands of the clock overlap).

Both intratextuality and intertextuality characterize Sokolov's work. Intertextuality reaffirms the idea of universal connection by linking hypertext and hypotext, modifying the latter by inserting it into the new context of the former. The result is a complex network of 'palimpsests', according to Genette's definition, in which different and yet somehow similar texts, such as parents and children, find themselves united across epochs, nations, linguistic and cultural environments. It is not necessary that the source code be the same as the target code: even different arts can be connected by intertextual relationships. Ekphrasis is indeed natural for the true artist, who does not recognize boundaries between the various forms of art: the existence of boundaries between them would limit artistic communication. What would Alexander Blok's poetry be if deprived of the lexicon offered by painting and music? The same can be said of Sokolov's work, in which not only does the ekphrastic reference to Bruegel's paintings play an important role, but so do also the countless references to music—we can think of, for instance, the "student so-and-so" merging with waltz music before his metamorphosis into a water lily, or of Palisandr comparing the existence to some piano sheet music. The idea of the natural interconnection and 'trespassing' of boundaries between genres and arts is explored in Chapter 4, which aims to find an appropriate definition for Sasha Sokolov's neologism *proeziia*—the macro-genre which fits what I have called 'Sokolovian baroqueness'.

In its pursuit of Beauty, art is no less capable than 'scientific' discourses of speaking about everything. Only, it does so in its own way, in forms that are not always transparent: "seemingly about something else, but essentially about this exactly" (I: 45), and sometimes even "silently" (III: 4) like the Hispanic lady does in *Philornist*. Art's ways may appear enigmatic, sibylline, similar to Zen stories, to haiku poems or to their 'predecessor' *renga*, a form of Japanese poetry that is known and admired by Sasha Sokolov:

> Soon, all progressive humanity will celebrate the seven hundredth anniversary of the birth of the greatest expert of this genre Nijō Yoshimoto [1320-1388], who wrote that the renga with its concatenated stanzas expresses the general connection of things. Philosophers of different ages have written and spoken about this, about the connection of things, see a whole heap of articles on this subject on the internet. Once, in my teens, I came up with this idea on my own, and it fits perfectly into my worldview and texts, and in *Triptych* it is like a fish in water, I would even say that there, in this thing, that is the main idea.[131]

Art speaks in an obscure, synthetic, and yet precise manner—in *Triptych*, the Venetian heron is called by its scientific name, *botaurus stellaris*[132] (III: 89). One must know how to listen to art's speech. It may reveal as much as science does, if not more, about the Beauty of the world, about its creatures, and phenomena.

The discourse on method that is the main subject of *Triptych*'s first section revolves around the principle of enumeration, present in both Cartesian and Baconian thought. However, Sokolov seems to mock the former, embracing a polemically anti-sectarian idea of the sciences and art. Perhaps it is instead Bacon's tables that become the term of reference and the starting point of the lists drawn up by *Triptich*'s voices. Alternatively, or at the same time, it is the thought of Comenius, who, starting from the work of the English philosopher and taking from him the idea of direct knowledge, reworked this notion and elaborated the 'syncritical method'. The Bohemian philosopher defined it as the analogical procedure that leads to the identification of the laws governing different phenomena and, more generally, to *Pansophia* (universal wisdom). The possibility to acquire knowledge through the identification of analogies between different elements seems to be an idea shared by *Triptych*'s voices.

In the meticulous enumeration compiled by these voices, every phenomenon, thing, creature finds its place, and every truth admits its opposite, as different ideas and positions are collected: such a polyphonic reasoning repudiates unitary and monological visions of the world. The positions are all internally linked, or they can be interpreted as different variations of the same idea. Indeed, the same

---

[131] Personal communication, email, July 3, 2019.

[132] It is possible that the choice of this animal is due to its scientific name's veiled reference to astronomy, a discipline mentioned several times in the text.

can be said for animal species: birds and (winged) insects share the same fundamental characteristics, just as the dog was mistaken for a wolf in Sokolov's second novel. In this sense, twilight, being a primary device in Sokolov's *proeziia*, serves as an instrument of defamiliarization: it allows the harmonious union of what appears incommensurable and opposite. This is, in the end, the essence of that absolute Beauty that, Sasha Sokolov finally asserts, humanity should pursue:

> Of science I, as they say, do not know much, I have never had any reason either to love it or to rely on it, unlike art. It seems to me that if mankind has any mission, then this is the creation of finesse (*iziashchnoe*)—not mountains of garbage, not the invention of all these gadgets, not the increase in the number of our kind, not the endless devouring of food, in short, not life itself. Art has always been there, through it we know ourselves and our surroundings, and it, certainly, explains many things to those who have ears and eyes. I do not know if these motifs can be heard in *Triptych*, looking from the outside you can see better, the cards are in your hand, fantasize and soar.[133]

---

[133] Personal communication, email, July 3, 2019.

References

Albanese 2017, *Procedimenti poetici in prosa: dinamiche sperimentali nella letteratura underground degli anni '60 e '70*, Doctoral dissertation, Università degli Studi di Roma "Tor Vergata".

Aleksandrov 2017, *Shkola dlia umnykh*, «Lenta.ru», 09/02/2017, https://lenta.ru/articles/2017/02/09/sokolov/.

Aitmatov 1989, *Na anketu "IL" otvechaiut pisateli russkogo zarubezh'ia. Sasha Sokolov*, «Inostrannaia Literatura», 3, pp. 245-246.

Aleinikov 1989, *Ochishchaiushshii SMOG*, «Molodoi kommunist», 8, pp. 79-89.

Bakhtin 1965, *Tvorchestvo Fransua Rable i narodnaia kul'tura srednevekov'ia i Renessansa*, Moskva, Khudozhestvennaia literatura.

Bakhtin 1975, *Voprosy literatury i estetiki*, Moskva, Khudozhestvennaia literatura.

Baknina 2015, *Sasha Sokolov i Piter Breigel' starshii: Dialog kul'tur*, «Literatura. Literaturovedenie. Ustnoe narodnoe tvorchestvo», III, 41, pp. 181-185.

Belting 2005, *Garden of Earthly Delights*, München, Prestel.

Berg 1985, *Novyi zhanr: Chitatel' i pisatel'*, «Literaturnoe A-Ja», 1, pp. 4-6.

Berg 1993, *Propushchennoe slovo: O tvorchestve Sashi Sokolova, zarubezhnogo pisatelia*, «Moskovskie novosti», 4, p. 7.

Boguslawski 1987, *Death in the Works of Sasha Sokolov*, «Canadian-American Slavic Studies», XXI, 3-4, pp. 231-246.

Boguslawski 2006, *How Sokolov's* Mezhdu sobakoi i volkom *is Made: Structure and Design*, «Canadian-American Slavic Studies», XL, 2-4, pp. 201-231.

Boguslawski 2012, *Introduction*, in S. Sokolov, *In the House of the Hanged: Essays and Vers Libres*, Toronto, University of Toronto Press, pp. vii-xx.

Borden 1987, *Time, Backward!: Sasha Sokolov and Valentin Kataev*, «Canadian-American Slavic Studies», XXI, 3-4, pp. 247-264.

Borisov 1990, *Non ci sarà la morte: genesi del Dottor Živago*, Milano, La casa di Matriona.

Bulgakov 2007, *A Dead Man's Memoir: A Theatrical Novel*, translated by Andrew Bromfield, London - New York, Penguin.

Canziani 1978 (ed.), *Come comunica il teatro*, Milano, Il formichiere.

Caramitti 2000, *Mul'tfil'm Breigelia i obraz Volgi v* Mezhdu sobakoi i volkom *Sashi Sokolova*, «Slavica Tergestina», 8, pp. 363-370.

Caramitti 2001, *Strategie autofinzionali in Sinjavskij, Sokolov e Venedikt Erofeev*, Doctoral dissertation, Università di Roma "La Sapienza".

Caramitti 2002, *Schegge di Russia,* Roma, Fanucci.

Caramitti 2004a, *Sokolov: il fabbro pellegrino della prosa russa*, «Il Manifesto», 15/12/2004, p. 12.

Caramitti 2004b, *Amore e morte sotto l'incudine di Saša Sokolov: l'incubo polimorfo, endemico e misterioso di "ta dama"*, in H. Pessina Longo, G. Imposti, D. Possamai (eds.), *Amore ed eros nella letteratura russa del Novecento. III Conferenza sulla letteratura russa del Novecento*, Bologna, Clueb, pp. 113-120.

Caramitti 2006, *"Ja" kak igrovoe nachalo iskusstva (po materialam* Palisandrii*)*, «Canadian-American Slavic Studies», XL, 2-4, pp. 305-315.

Caramitti 2019, *Palisandr dentro e fuori la vasca*, in S. Sokolov, *Palissandreide*, translated by Mario Caramitti, Roma, Atmosphere, pp. 405-429.

Chantsev 2012, *Slovo c Berega Odinokogo Kozodoia*, «Novy mir», 2.

Cherednichenko 2012, *Po tropinkam vnutrennego sada*, «Znamia», 10, http://magazines.russ.ru/znamia/2012/10/ch17.html.

Danilov 2017, Shkola dlia durakov *Sashi Sokolova glazami avtora* Gorizontal'nogo polozheniia *Dmitriia Danilova*, «godliteratury.ru», https://godliteratury.ru/public-post/sasha-sokolov-shkola-dlya-durakov.

Dark 1990, *Mir mozhet byt' liuboi: Razmyshleniia o novoi proze*, «Druzhba narodov», 6, pp. 223-235.

Dark 1992, *Mif o proze*, «Druzhba narodov», 5-6, pp. 219-232.

De Jonge 1976, *A Dacha for the Demented*, «Times Literary Supplement», 27/08/1976.

Divakov 2013, *Poznavshii prirodu tetivy. O rannem tvorchestve Sashi Sokolova*, «Voprosy literatury», 1, http://magazines.russ.ru/voplit/2013/1/d5-pr.html.

Egorov 2012a, *Smyslovaia neopredelyonnost' v* Gazibo *Sashi Sokolova*, «Iaroslavskii pedagogicheskii vestnik», 3, pp. 189-194.

Egorov 2012b, *Nartsissicheskaia povestvovatel'naia struktura* Filornita *Sashi Sokolova*, «Iaroslavskii pedagogicheskii vestnik», 4, pp. 222-226.

Egorov 2013, *Aktualizatsiia metateksta v* Rassuzhdenii *Sashi Sokolova*, «Iaroslavskii pedagogicheskii vestnik», 3, pp. 181-185.

Elam 2005, *The Semiotics of Theatre and Drama*, London - New York, Routledge.

Erofeev 1989, *Sokolov: "Vremia dlia chastnykh besed"*, «Oktiabr'», 8, pp. 195-202.

Freedman 1987, *Memory, Imagination and the Liberating Force of Literature in Sasha Sokolov's* A School for Fools, «Canadian-American Slavic Studies», XXI, 3-4, pp. 265-278.

Gasparov 1993, *Russkie stikhi 1890-1925 godov v kommentariiakh*, Moskva, Vysshaia shkola.

Gasparov 1996, *A History of European Versification*, translated by G.S. Smith and Marina Tarlinskaya, Oxford, Clarendon Press.

Greenberg 1977, *A School for Fools*, «New York Times Book Review», 25/09/1977, p. 41.

Groys 1987, *Zhizn' kak utopiia i utopiia kak zhizn': Iskusstvo soc-arta*, «Sintaksis», 18, pp. 171-181.

Groys 2013 (ed.), *Utopiia i real'nost': El' Lisitskii, Il'ia i Emiliia Kabakovy*, Sankt Peterburg, Gosudarstvennyi Ermitazh.

Gulin 2011, *Smert'iu iziashchnykh*, «colta.ru», http://os.colta.ru/literature/projects/30291/details/32247.

Gureev 2011, *Snimaetsia dokumental'noe kino: Sasha Sokolov*, «Voprosy literatury», 2, pp. 161-172.

Heldt 1987, *Female Skaz in Sasha Sokolov's* Between Dog and Wolf, «Canadian-American Slavic Studies», XXI, 3-4, pp. 279-286.

Iablokov 1997, *«Nashel ia nachalo dorogi otsiuda – tuda» (O motivnoi strukture romana Sashi Sokolova* Mezhdu sobakoi i volkom*)*, in V. Skobelev (ed.), *Literatura tret'ei volny*, Samara, Izd-vo Samarskogo universiteta, pp. 202-214.

Ingold 1979, Škola dlja durakov. *Versuch über Saša Sokolov*, «Wiener Slawistischer Almanach», 3, pp. 93-124.

Jakobson 1966, *Grammatical Parallelism and Russian Facet*, «Language», XLII, 2, pp. 399-429.

Jakobson 1990, *Language in Literature*, Boston, Belknap Press.

Jo 1976, *Sasha Sokolov's in from the Cold, with his Sense of Humour Intact and a Powerful Yen to Write*, «Detroit Free Press», 05/12/1976, pp. 21-24.

Johnson 1980, *A Structural Analysis of Sasha Sokolov's* School for Fools*: A Paradigmatic Novel*, in Birnbaum H., Eekman T. (eds.), *Fiction and Drama in Eastern and Southeastern Europe: Evolution and Experiment in the Postwar Period*, Columbus, Slavica, pp. 207-237.

Johnson 1982, Mezhdu sobakoi i volkom*: O fantasticheskom iskusstve Sashi Sokolova*, «Vremia i my», 64, pp. 165-175.

Johnson 1984, *Sasha Sokolov's* Between Dog and Wolf *and the Modernist Tradition*, in O. Matich, M. Heim (eds.), *Russian Literature in Emigration: The Third Wave*, Ann Arbor, Ardis, pp. 208-217.

Johnson 1986a, *Sasha Sokolov's Twilight Cosmos: Themes and Motifs*, «Slavic Review», 45, pp. 639-649.

Johnson 1986b, *Sasha Sokolov's* Palisandriia, «Slavic and East European Journal», XXX, 3, pp. 389-403.

Johnson 1987a, *Sasha Sokolov: A Literary Biography*, «Canadian-American Slavic Studies», XXI, 3-4, pp. 203-230.

Johnson 1987b, *Sasha Sokolov and Vladimir Nabokov*, «Russian Language Journal», XLI, 138-139, pp. 153-162

Johnson 1989, *Sasha Sokolov: The New Russian Avant-Garde*, «Critique: Studies in Modern Fiction», XXX, 3, pp. 163-178.

Johnson 2006, *Sasha Sokolov's Major Essays*, «Canadian-American Slavic Studies», XL, 2-4, pp. 233-249.

Karriker 1979, *Double Vision: Sasha Sokolov's* School for Fools, «World Literature Today», 3, pp. 610-614.

Katsov 2017, *Mezhdu sudoku i voplem. O Sashe Sokolove, mastere plesti intrigu*, «Znamia», 8, http://literaryamerica.ru/almanakh/pub/mezhdu-sudoku-i-voplem.html.

Kislov 2012, *Repetitsiia reinkarnatsii*, «Novoe Literaturnoe Obozrenie», 113, http://magazines.russ.ru/nlo/2012/113/k38.html#_ftnref17.

Knight 2006, *How the Cold War Began: The Igor Gouzenko Affair and the Hunt for Soviet Spies*, New York, Carroll & Graf.

Kochetkova 2017, *"Ia vsegda znal, chto uedu iz Sovetskogo Soiuza"*, «Lenta.ru», https://lenta.ru/articles/2017/02/11/sokolovfilm/.

Komarova 2013, *Retsepstiia tvorchestva Sashi Sokolova v kritike russkogo zarubezh'ia 1970-1980-kh godov*, «Filologicheskie nauki: Voprosy teorii i praktiki», 28, pp. 85-89.

Kopeikin 1985, *Bezotchetnyi soldat istorii: o novom romane Sashi Sokolova*, «Russkaia mysl'», 27/09/1985, p. 15.

Kormiłow 2011, *Ritmicheskaia, metrizovannaia i rifmovannaia proza v romanakh Sashi Sokolova*, «Polilog. Studia Neofilologiczne», 1, pp. 67-75.

Kreid 1981, *Zaitil'shchina*, «Dvadtsat' dva», 19, pp. 213-218.

Krokhin 1992, *Profili na serebre: Povest' o Leonide Gubanove*, Moskva, Obnovlenie.

Kucherskaya 2011, *Po chasti rechi*, «Vedomosti», 06/10/2011, 2871, http://www.vedomosti.ru/newspaper/articles/2011/06/1 0/po_chasti_rechi.

Kuritsyn 2000, *Russkii literaturnyi postmodernizm*, Moskva, OGI.

Leiderman, Lipovetsky 2003, *Sovremennaia russkaia literatura: 1950-1990-e gody*, Moskva, Akademiia.

Lepakhin 2007, *Ikona i obraz, ikonichnost' i slovesnost'*, Moskva, Palomnik.

Likhachev 2009, *Russkoe iskusstvo*, Sankt Peterburg, Iskusstvo.

Lipovetsky 1995, *Mifologiia metamorfoz: Poetika* Shkoly dlia durakov *Sashi Sokolova*, «Oktjabr'», 7, pp. 183-192.

Lipovetsky 1997, *Russkii postmodernizm (Ocherki istoricheskoi poetiki)*, Ekaterinburg, Ural'skii gosudarstvennyi pedagogicheskii universitet.

Lipovetsky 1999, *Russian Postmodernist Fiction. Dialogue with Chaos*, Armonk – New York – London, M.E. Sharpe.

Litus 1997, *Saša Sokolov's* Škola dlja durakov*: Aesopian Language and Intertextual Play*, «Slavic and East European Journal», XLI, 1, pp. 114-134.

Litus 2006, *Sasha Sokolov's Journey from Samizdat to Russia's Favorite Classic*, «Canadian-American Slavic Studies», XL, 2-4, pp. 393-424.

Lorca 1922, *La importancia histórica y artística del primitivo canto andaluz, llamado cante jondo*, https://verseando.com/blog/lorca-el-cante-jondo/.

Marchesini 2012a, *Per un recupero della iziashchnaia slovesnost': osservazioni sul linguaggio proetico di Saša Sokolov*, «Slavica Tergestina», 14, pp. 38-77.

Marchesini 2012b, *Il personaggio scontornato in* Škola dlja durakov*. Dal romanzo di Saša Sokolov agli adattamenti teatrali*, «Between», II, 4, pp. 1-19.

Marchesini 2018a, *Lo specchio del tempo: la permanenza del retaggio linguistico-culturale anticorusso nella prosa russa contemporanea*, Roma, UniversItalia.

Marchesini 2018b, *Levigati dall'assenza: la costruzione del personaggio nella prosa metafinzionale russo-sovietica*, Roma, UniversItalia.

Matich 1984, *Interview*, «Humanities in Society», VII, 3-4, pp. 221-234.

Matich 1985a, *"Nuzhno zabyt' vse staroe i vspomnit' vse novoe"*, «Russkaia mysl'», 31/05/1985, p. 12.

Matich 1985b, Palisandriia*: Dissidentskii mif i ego razvenchanie*, «Sintaksis», 15, pp. 86-102.

Matich 1986, *Sasha Sokolov's* Palisandriia: *History and Myth*, «The Russian Review», 45, pp. 415-426.

Matich 1987, *Sasha Sokolov and His Literary Context*, «Canadian-American Slavic Studies», XXI, 3-4, pp. 301-319.

Matich 2017, *Neobarochnaia* Palisandriia: *vremia, al'ternativnaia istoriia, pamiat'*, «Novyi zhurnal», 289, http://magazines.russ.ru/nj/2017/289/neobarochnaya-palisandriya-sashi-sokolova-vremya-alternativnaya.html.

Matveev 2015, *Palisandrovo vremia. Tridtsat' let tomu nazad vyshel roman Sashi Sokolova* Palisandriia, «colta.ru», 01/04/2015, http://www.colta.ru/articles/literature/6812.

McMillin 1990, *Aberration or the Future: The Avant-Garde Novels of Sasha Sokolov*, in Id. (ed.), *From Pushkin to* Palisandriia: *Essays on the Russian Novel*, London, School of Slavonic and East European Studies – University of London, pp. 229-243.

Meynet 2012, *Treatise on Biblical Rhetoric*, Boston, Brill.

Mss 117, *Sasha Sokolov Collection*, University of California Santa Barbara, USA, Davidson Library, Department of Special Collections (9 Document Boxes, 13 Audiocassettes).

Nabokov 1971, *Ada or Ardor: A Family Chronicle*, London, Penguin.

Napolitano 2018, *Il principio ekphrastico nel quadro proetico di Saša Sokolov*, in E. Dammiano, E. Gironi Carnevale, E. Mari, O. Trukhanova (eds.), *(S)confinamenti. Rapporti fra letteratura e arti figurative in area slava*, Roma, UniversItalia, pp. 199-212.

Napolitano 2020a, *Tracce di SMOG: un "ritratto di gruppo" affrescato da Saša Sokolov. A proposito di* Obščaja tetrad' *(1989)*, «Between», 19, pp. 307-332.

Napolitano 2020b, *Meeting the Duende: Sasha Sokolov reads Federico García Lorca*, «eSamizdat», 13, pp. 375-381.

Napolitano 2021, *Simfoniia iazyka:* Triptikh *Sashi Sokolova i ego muzykal'nye motivy*, «Voprosy literatury», 3, pp. 124-148.

Nolting-Hauff 1959, *Die Stellung der Liebeskasuistik im höfischen Roman*, Heidelberg, Carl Winter.

Orlitsky 1991, *Stikh i proza v russkoi literature. Ocherki istorii i teorii*, Voronezh, VGU.

Orlitsky 1997, *Stikhovoe nachalo v proze "tret'ei volny"*, in V. Skobelev (ed.), *Literatura "tret'ei volny"*, Samara, Samarskii universitet, pp. 44-54.

Orlitsky 2002, *Stikh i proza v russkoi literature*, Moskva, RGGU.

Orlitsky 2008, *Dinamika stikha i prozy v russkoi slovesnosti*, Moskva, RGGU.

Orobii 2012, *Istoriia odnogo uchenichestva (Vladimir Nabokov – Sasha Sokolov – Mikhail Shishkin)*, «Novoe Literaturnoe Obozrenie», 118, http://www.intelros.ru/readroom/nlo/118-2012/17388-istoriya-odnogo-uchenichestva-vladimir-nabokov-sasha-sokolov-mihail-shishkin.html.

Ostanin 2020, *Slovar' k povesti Sashi Sokolova* Mezhdu sobakoi i volkom, Sankt Peterburg, Pal'mira.

Pagnini 1974, *Lingua e musica*, Bologna, Il Mulino.

Pascal 1995, *Pensées*, London, Penguin.

Perel'man 1986, *Po stranicam zhurnalov "22" i "Sintaksis": Somnitel'naia mifologiia*, «Vremia i my», 91, pp. 181-193.

Persi 1999, *I suoni incrociati. Poeti e musicisti nella Russia romantica*, Viareggio, Mauro Baroni.

Podshivalov 2006, *A Conversation with Sasha Sokolov: Moscow, 1989*, «Canadian-American Slavic Studies», XL, 2-4, pp. 352-366.

Polovets, Rakhlin 1981, *Sasha Sokolov govorit*, «almanac panorama», 03/09/1981, pp. 8-12.

Pomerantsev 2013, *Sasha Sokolov o Khlebnikove*, «Radio Svoboda», http://www.svoboda.org/a/25161164.html.

Possamai 2004, *Sulla critica del postmodernismo: spunti di riflessione*, «Studi slavistici», 1, pp. 115-125.

RLJ 1977, *Shkola dlia durakov*, «Russian Language Journal», 108, pp. 188-193.

Rudova 2000a, *Paradigms of Postmodernism: Conceptualism and Sots-Art in Contemporary Russian Literature*, «Pacific Coast Philology», XXXV, 1, pp. 61-75.

Rudova 2000b, *Reading* Palisandriia*: Of Menippean Satire and Sots-Art*, in M. Balina, N. Condee, E. Dobrenko (eds.), *End-Quote: Sots-Art Literature and Soviet Grand Style*, Evanston, Northwestern University Press, pp. 211- 224.

Rudova 2006, *The Dystopian Vision in Sasha Sokolov's* Palisandriia, «Canadian-American Slavic Studies», XL, 2-4, pp. 163-177.

Salomatin, Skvortsov 2021, Mezhdu sobakoi i volkom *kak osevoi tekst v pisatel'skom universume Sashi Sokolova*, «Canadian-American Slavic Studies», LV, 4, forthcoming.

Shchuplov 1988, *Tatyana Tolstaya: "Poidite navstrechu chitateliu"*, «Knizhnoe obozrenie», 1, p. 4.

Segre 1984, *Teatro e romanzo*, Torino, Einaudi.

Seltzer 1977, *Sowing the Wind*, «The Word Guild», II, 8, p. 17.

Schlögel 2016, *In Space We Read Time: On the History of Civilisation and Geopolitics*, translated by Gerrit Jackson, New York, Bard Graduate Center.

Shatin 2013, *Kurs diskursa v* Triptikhe *Sashi Sokolova: ot ritoriki k poetike*, «Kritika i semiotika», XVIII, 1, pp. 200-208.

Simmons 1989, *Incarnation of the Hero Archetype in* School for fools, in A. Mandelker, R. Reeder (eds.), *The Supernatural in Slavic and Baltic Literature: Essays in Honor of Victor Terras*, Columbus, Slavica, pp. 275-289.

Simmons 1993, *Their Fathers' Voice: Vassily Aksyonov, Venedikt Erofeev, Eduard Limonov and Sasha Sokolov*, Bern - New York, Peter Lang.

Skoropanova 1999, *Russkaia postmodernistskaia proza*, Moskva, Flint-Nauka.

Skvortsov 2018, *Iavivshiesia v inom oblichii*, «Oktiabr'», 9, http://www.intelros.ru/readroom/oktyabr/o9-2018/36755-yavivshiesya-v-inom-oblichii.html.

Slepynin 2007, *Sasha Sokolov na fone Karadaga i vinogradnoi lozy*, «Zerkalo nedeli», 26/10/2007, https://zn.ua/SOCIUM/sasha_sokolov_na_fone_karadaga_i_vinogradnoy_lozy.html.

Smith 1987, *The Verse in Sasha Sokolov's* Between Dog and Wolf, «Canadian-American Slavic Studies», XXI, 3-4, pp. 321-345.

Sokolov 1971, *Poznat' prirodu tetivy: Mariiskie poety*, «Literaturnaia gazeta», 10/09/1971, p. 18.

Sokolov 1977, *Tekst*, «Glagol», 1, pp. 7-24.

Sokolov 1989, *Astrophobia*, translated by Michael Henry Heim, New York, Grove Weidenfeld.

Sokolov 1999, *Sobranie sochinenii v dvukh tomakh*, Saint Petersburg, Simpozium.

Sokolov 2006, *Duende*, «Zerkalo», 28, http://zerkalo-litart.com/?p=1455.

Sokolov 2011, *Triptikh*, Moskva, OGI.

Sokolov 2012, *In the House of the Hanged: Essays and Vers Libres*, translated by Alexander Boguslawski, Toronto, University of Toronto Press.

Sokolov 2014, *Ozarenie*, «Oktiabr'», 10, pp. 14-15.

Sokolov 2015, *A School for Fools*, translated by Alexander Boguslawski, New York, New York Review Books.

Sokolov 2017, *Between Dog and Wolf*, translated by Alexander Boguslawski, New York, Columbia University Press.

Sokolov 2020, *Shkola dlia durakov. Mezhdu sobakoi i volkom. Palisandriia. Triptikh. Esse*, Sankt Peterburg, Azbooka.

von Ssachno 1979, *Valentin Katajew und Sascha Sokolow*, in G. Lindemann (ed.), *Sowjetliteratur Heute*, München, Beck, pp. 208-218.

Ternovsky 1980, *Sostav prozy (Novaia povest' Sashi Sokolova)*, «Russkaia mysl'», 26/06/1980, p. 13.

Todorov 1976, *Introduction à la littérature phantastique*, Paris, Seuil.

Toker 1987, *Gamesman's Sketches (Found in a Bottle): A Reading of Sasha Sokolov's Between Dog and Wolf*, «Canadian-American Slavic Studies», XXI, 3-4, pp. 347-367.

Tolstaya 1988, *Vstupitel'noe slovo k publikatsii otryvka iz romana Sashi Sokolova* Shkola dlia durakov, «Ogoniok», 33, pp. 20-21.

Toporov 2009, *Russkii Agasfer. U Sashi Sokolova net Boga, net Otechestva, net Liubvi. Tol'ko stil'*, «Chastnyi korrespondent», http://www.chaskor.ru/article/russkij_agasfer_11974.

Tumanov 1994, *A Tale Told by Two Idiots – Krik idiota v* Shkole dlia durakov *Sashi Sokolova i* Shume i jarosti *Uil'iama Folknera*, «Russian Language Journal», 48, pp. 137-154.

Tynyanov 1929, *O literaturnoi evolutsii*, in *Arkhaisty i novatory*, Leningrad, Priboi, pp. 30-47.

UArch FacP 60, *Johnson Papers 1970-2010*, University of California Santa Barbara, USA, Davidson Library, Department of Special Collections (17 Document Boxes, 8 Audiocassettes).

Vail', Genis 1980, *Literaturnye mechtaniia*, «Chast' rechi», 1, pp. 204-233.

Vail', Genis 1986a, *U nas v Michigane*, «almanac panorama», 16/05/1986, 265, pp. 20-22.

Vail', Genis 1986b, *Tsvetnik rossiiskogo anakhronizma. Soslagatel'noe naklonenie istorii*, «Grani», 139, pp. 159-164.

Vail', Genis 1993, *Uroki shkoly dlia durakov: O romane Sashi Sokolova* Shkola dlia durakov, «Literaturnoe obozrenie», 1, pp. 13-16.

Vaiman 2003, *Poverkh bar'erov. Beseda s Sashei Sokolovym*, «Radio Svoboda», http://www.svoboda.org/a/24200193.html.

Vedomosti 1996, *Sasha Sokolov – laureat Pushkinskoi premii fonda Al'freda Tepfera*, «Vedomosti», 10/02/1996, p. 13.

Veidle 1976, *Begstvo v nevmeniaemost'*, «Russkaia mysl'», 3100, p. 10.

Vergara 2021, *Flap Your Wings for Goodbye: Sasha Sokolov's Bird Imagery in* Between Dog and Wolf, «Canadian-American Slavic Studies», LV, 4, forthcoming.

Vrubel'-Golubkina 2011, *Sokolov: "Ia vsiu zhizn' vybiraiu luchshee. Chashche vsego bessoznatel'no"*, «Zerkalo», 37-38, https://magazines.gorky.media/zerkalo/2011/37/ya-vsyu-zhizn-vybirayu-luchshee-chashhe-vsego-bessoznatelno-8230.html.

Witte 1989, *Text als Spiel – Saša Sokolovs* Škola dlja durakov, in Id., *Appell – Spiel – Ritual. Textpraktiken in der russischen Literatur der sechziger bis achtziger Jahre*, Wiesbaden, Harassowitz, pp. 93-144.

Zholkovsky 1987, *The Stylistic Roots of* Palisandriia, «Canadian-American Slavic Studies», XXI, 3-4, pp. 369-400, https://dornsife.usc.edu/alexander-zholkovsky/palissandria.

Ziolkowski 1987, *In the Land of the Lonely Goatsucker: Ornithic Imagery in* A School for Fools *and* Between Dog and Wolf, «Canadian-American Slavic Studies», XXI, 3-4, pp. 401-416.

Zorin 1989, *Nasylaiushchii veter*, «Novy mir», 12, pp. 250-253.

Literatur und Kultur im mittleren und östlichen Europa

herausgegeben von Reinhard Ibler

ISSN 2195-1497

1   *Elisa-Maria Hiemer*
    Generationenkonflikt und Gedächtnistradierung
    Die Aufarbeitung des Holocaust in der polnischen Erzählprosa des 21.
    Jahrhunderts
    ISBN 978-3-8382-0394-2

2   *Adam Jarosz*
    Przybyszewski und Japan
    Bezüge und Annäherungen
    Mit einem Vorwort von Hanna Ratuszna und Quellentexten in Erstübertragung
    ISBN 978-3-8382-0436-9

3   *Adam Jarosz*
    Das Todesmotiv im Drama von Stanisław Przybyszewski
    ISBN 978-3-8382-0496-3

4   *Valentina Kaptayn*
    Zwischen Tabu und Trauma
    Kateřina Tučkovás Roman *Vyhnání Gerty Schnirch* im Kontext der
    tschechischen Literatur über die Vertreibung der Deutschen
    ISBN 978-3-8382-0482-6

5   *Reinhard Ibler (Hg.)*
    Der Holocaust in den mitteleuropäischen
    Literaturen und Kulturen seit 1989
    The Holocaust in the Central European Literatures and Cultures since 1989
    ISBN 978-3-8382-0512-0

6   *Iris Bauer*
    Schreiben über den Holocaust
    Zur literarischen Kommunikation in Marian Pankowskis Erzählung *Nie ma
    Żydówki*
    ISBN 978-3-8382-0587-8

7   *Olga Zitová*
    Thomas Mann und Ivan Olbracht
    Der Einfluss von Manns Mythoskonzeption auf die karpatoukrainische Prosa
    des tschechischen Schriftstellers
    ISBN 978-3-8382-0633-2

8   *Trixi Jansen*
    Der Tod und das Mädchen
    Eine Analyse des Paradigmas aus Tod und Weiblichkeit in ausgewählten
    Erzählungen I.S. Turgenev
    ISBN 978-3-8382-0627-1

9   *Olena Sivuda*
    "Aber plötzlich war mir, als drohe das Haus über mir
    zusammenzubrechen."
    Komparative Analyse des Heimkehrermotivs in der deutschen und russischen
    Prosa nach dem Zweiten Weltkrieg
    ISBN 978-3-8382-0779-7

10 *Victoria Oldenburger*
    Keine Menschen, sondern ganz besondere Wesen ...
    Die Frau als Objekt unkonventioneller Faszination in Ivan A. Bunins Erzählband
    Temnye allei (1937–1949)
    ISBN 978-3-8382-0777-3

11 *Andrea Meyer-Fraatz, Thomas Schmidt (Hg.)*
    „Ich kann es nicht fassen,
    dass dies Menschen möglich ist"
    Zur Rolle des Emotionalen in der polnischen Literatur
    über den Holocaust
    ISBN 978-3-8382-0859-6

12 *Julia Friedmann*
    Von der Gorbimanie zur Putinphobie?
    Ursachen und Folgen medialer Politisierung
    ISBN 978-3-8382-0936-4

13 *Reinhard Ibler (Hg.)*
    Der Holocaust in den mitteleuropäischen Literaturen und Kulturen:
    Probleme der Politisierung und Ästhetisierung
    The Holocaust in the Central European Literatures and Cultures:
    Problems of Poetization and Aestheticization
    ISBN 978-3-8382-0952-4

14 *Alexander Lell*
    Studien zum erzählerischen Schaffen Vsevolod M. Garšins
    Zur Betrachtung des Unrechts in seinen Werken aus der Willensperspektive
    Arthur Schopenhauers
    ISBN 978-3-8382-1042-1

15   *Dmitry Shlapentokh*
     The Mongol Conquests in the Novels of Vasily Yan
     An Intellectual Biography
     ISBN 978-3-8382-1017-9

16   *Katharina Bauer*
     Liebe – Glaube – Russland:
     Russlandkonzeptionen im Schaffen Aleksej N. Tolstojs
     ISBN 978-3-8382-1182-4

17   *Magdalena Baran-Szołtys, Monika Glosowitz,*
     Aleksandra Konarzewska (eds.)
     Imagined Geographies
     Central European Spatial Narratives between 1984 and 2014
     ISBN 978-3-8382-1225-8

18   *Adam Jarosz*
     Der Spiegel und die Spiegelungen
     Über Geschlecht und Seele im Werk von Stanisław Przybyszewski
     ISBN 978-3-8382-1246-3

19   *Šárka Sladovníková*
     The Holocaust in Czechoslovak
     and Czech Feature Films
     ISBN 978-3-8382-1196-1

20   *Julia Spanberger*
     Grenzen und Grenzerfahrungen in den Texten Viktor Pelevins
     Eine Analyse seiner frühen Prosa
     ISBN 978-3-8382-1460-3

21   *Magda Dolińska-Rydzek*
     The Antichrist in Post-Soviet Russia: Transformations of an Ideomyth
     ISBN 978-3-8382-1545-7

22   *Martina Napolitano*
     Sasha Sokolov: The Life and Work of the Russian "Proet"
     ISBN 978-3-8382-1619-5

ibidem.eu